LEADERSHIP:
AN ISLAMIC PERSPECTIVE

First Edition
(1999 A.C. / 1420 A.H.)

*This book is dedicated to our parents
and to a leader who has inspired
many: Khurram Murad.*

وَ جَعَلْنَـٰهُمْ أَئِمَّةً يَهْدُونَ بِأَمْرِنَا وَ أَوْحَيْنَآ إِلَيْهِمْ فِعْلَ
الْخَيْرَٰتِ وَإِقَامَ الصَّلَوٰةِ وَإِيتَآءَ الزَّكَوٰةِ ۖ وَكَانُواْ لَنَا
عَـٰبِدِينَ

And We made them leaders guiding (men) by Our
Command and We sent them inspiration to do good
deeds, to establish regular prayers and to practice
regular charity; and they constantly served Us (and
Us only). (Anbiyaa, 21:73)*

* The Qur'an is the last of the divine books revealed by God (Allah) to
His last messenger, the Prophet Muhammad (peace be upon him). All
Qur'an citations in this book will be followed in parentheses by *surah*
(chapter), *surah* number and *ayat* (verse).

LEADERSHIP: AN ISLAMIC PERSPECTIVE

Rafik I. Beekun

and

Jamal Badawi

amana publications
Beltsville, Maryland

1420 A.H. / 1999 A.C. by
amana publications
10710 Tucker Street
Beltsville, Maryland 20705-2223 USA
Tel: (301)595-5777 Fax: (301)595-5888
Email: igamana@erols.com, www.amana-publications.com

Library of Congress Cataloging-in-Publication Data

Beekun, Rafik Issa.
    Leadership, an Islamic perspective / Rafik I. Beekun and Jamal
Badawi.
    p. cm.
    Includes bibliographical references (p.   ) and index.
    ISBN 0-91-595794-9
    1. Leadership--Religious aspects--Islam. 2. Management--Religious
aspects--Islam. 3. Islamic ethics. I. Badawi, Jamal A. II. Title.
    BP190.5.L4B44 1999
    297.6'1--dc21
                                                            99-42025
                                                                CIP

Printed in the United States of America by International Graphics
10710 Tucker Street
Beltsville, Maryland 20705-2223 USA
Tel. (301)595-5999 Fax (301)595-5888
Email: igfx@aol.com

Contents

Preface

In the Name of Allah,[1] The Beneficent, The Merciful

Leadership in Islam is a trust (*amānah*). It represents a psychological contract between a leader and his followers that he will try his best to guide them, to protect them, and to treat them justly. Hence, the focus of leadership in Islam is on doing good.

According to Islam, every person is the "shepherd" of a flock, and occupies a position of leadership.[2] *Leadership: An Islamic Perspective* is about how Muslims[3] enact their leadership role. This book is directed at both non-Muslims seeking to understand the leadership paradigm of one billion Muslims globally and at Muslims wishing to understand leadership better.

Why should you be interested in leadership from an Islamic perspective? Here are some new global facts that relate specifically to the renaissance that Muslims are currently experiencing:

Muslims are waking up. Look around you. Muslims are coming back together. They are re-uniting. They are standing up for their rights — politically and otherwise. And they are succeeding. Recently, global corporations such as Nike and American Airlines have backed down in the face of the justified indignation of Muslims in America, and have removed offensive labels or rehired Muslims. Law enforcement agencies, public institutions and corporations in North America are now engaged in diversity training; in addition to other issues related to minorities, such programs attempt to educate employees about interaction with Muslims. These changes have happened because of the work of one Muslim organization, the Council on American-Islamic

---

[1] Allah or God. Allah is the personal name of God, the creator and sustainer of all.

[2] Reported by 'Abd Allah ibn 'Umar, *Sahih Bukhari*, hadith 3.733. The term "hadith" refers to the sayings and actions of the Prophet Muhammad (*saw*).

[3] The term "Muslim" is used throughout the book in its generic meaning to include both males and females who submit their will to Allah. All Islamic and/or Arabic terms are explained in the glossary on page 135.

Relations (CAIR). With the help of the Muslim community in North America, CAIR has succeeded in turning back the tide of anti-Islamic coverage in the popular media. In Britain, the Muslim Council of Britain (MCB) has just recently been set up to coordinate the voices of all Muslims and Muslim organizations in Great Britain.

Muslims are becoming Ummah[4] *aware.* The rise of regional, and even global, Muslim-led or Muslim-owned Multinational Corporations (MNCs) such as Hicom (Malaysia), Savola (Saudi Arabia) or Infocom (USA) indicates that they can succeed at the global community or Ummah level. The information revolution has also helped Muslims become aware of their common destiny. When they wake up and see the faces of their raped sisters in Kosovo or the repression of a whole Muslim people in China, there is immediate empathy and anguish. In spite of the lukewarm efforts of their own governments, Muslims from many countries joined the Bosnians in their efforts to defend themselves against "ethnic cleansing."

Education and knowledge management are key. Muslims are beginning to invest heavily in education and knowledge management, and the results are tangible. The Pentium chip that powers millions of computers around the world had several Muslims on the development team. Professor Abdul Wahab El Messiri is one of the leading authorities in paradigm shifts. Safi Quraishi was one of the founders of AST, a globally known personal computer manufacter. The 1998 Noble Prize Winner for Medicine was Dr. Ferid Murad. Muslims are realizing that the true source of wealth is not exhaustible oil resources, but intellectual pre-eminence. This realization is leading Muslim countries around the world to invest in themselves and in the education of future generations on a massive scale. Malaysia, for example, is investing $40 billion dollars in developing a Multimedia Service Corridor to compete with America's Silicon Valley.

The leadership paradigm is changing, and ethics is making a comeback. The best sellers in the area of leadership now emphasize sincerity and integrity. The Machiavellian and other self-serving models of leadership which have long dominated contemporary thinking in this area are being dethroned. The House and Senate Committees on Ethics in the United States have been scrutinizing many lawmakers' business transactions and fundraising activities. The superiority of a leadership model centered on ethical principles is finally emerging — a position that Islam has embraced since its beginning.

---

[4] Ummah is an Islamic concept referring to a community of believers, regardless of race, ethnic background, or geographic location.

Democracy is on the rise, providing more people with the ability to explore and practice Islam. Whenever Muslims or non-Muslims are allowed more democracy, they are consistently choosing Islam. Decades of experimentation with alternate systems of government have been fruitless, and core Islamic values are reasserting themselves. Islam is the fastest growing religion in the United States, and is now the second largest religion in France.

We assume complete responsibility for all views expressed in this book. We apologize for any mistake that may have gone unnoticed. We would appreciate it if the copyrights to this book are not violated by either unauthorized reprinting or translation. Please contact us first for written permission.

Finally, we would like to acknowledge the superb contributions of Dr. Hisham Abdullah, Dr. Ahmad Sakr, and Dr. Iqbal Unus. We would also like to thank Dr. Khalid Iqbal, Amgad Hassan, Abbas Taylor, and Professor Nazir Ansari for their comments on the manuscript. During one five-hour international call, Khalid Ali, former president of the Federation of Student Islamic Societies (FOSIS) in the UK, provided thorough and extensive feedback to us. These reviewers provided us with detailed, constructive, and valuable suggestions. We have also learned much from the comments of the participants in our leadership workshops held throughout four continents. Nadiah Beekun read numerous versions of the manuscript and helped considerably during the whole process. Finally, we must acknowledge the posthumous contribution of Khurram Murad throughout this book.

Rafik I. Beekun   Jamal Badawi
University of Nevada   St. Mary's University
USA   Canada

July 12, 1999

Introduction
Leadership: An Islamic Perspective

أَهُمْ يَقْسِمُونَ رَحْمَتَ رَبِّكَ نَحْنُ قَسَمْنَا بَيْنَهُم مَّعِيشَتَهُمْ
فِى الْحَيَوٰةِ الدُّنْيَا وَرَفَعْنَا بَعْضَهُمْ فَوْقَ بَعْضٍ دَرَجَٰتٍ
لِيَتَّخِذَ بَعْضُهُم بَعْضًا سُخْرِيًّا وَرَحْمَتُ رَبِّكَ خَيْرٌ مِّمَّا
يَجْمَعُونَ

Is it they who would portion out the mercy of your
Lord? It is We who portion out between them their
livelihood in the life of this world: and We raise
some of them above others in ranks so that some
may command work from others. But the mercy of
your Lord is better than the (wealth) which they
amass. (Zukhruf, 43:32)

'Abd Allah ibn 'Umar (Allah be pleased with them) reported that the
Messenger of Allah (*saw*)[5] said: "Behold! Each of you is a guardian, and
each of you will be asked about his subjects. [...]" [6]

Objectives of This Book

After reading this book and doing the leadership exercises included
therein, you should, *in sha' Allah*,[7] be able to:

---

[5] *saw*: May the peace and mercy of Allah be upon him. This is a common phrase used by
Muslims whenever the name of the Prophet Muhammad is mentioned.

[6] *Sahih Bukhari*, hadith 3.733.

[7] God willing.

- Understand the nature and process of leadership from an Islamic perspective.
- Describe the characteristics of effective leaders in general, and of Islamic leaders in particular.
- Analyze your styles as a leader and follower.
- Learn how you can mobilize, organize, and develop your followers Islamically.
- Learn how you, as a leader, can build commitment by acting as a coach and mentor.
- Learn how to delegate effectively.
- Understand the steps that will enable you to become a more effective leader (or follower).

The subject of leadership is crucial in Islam. In most circumstances in life, Muslims are urged to appoint a leader and follow him. For example, the Prophet Muhammad (*saw*) said, "When three are on a journey, they should appoint one of them as their commander."[8] According to the Prophet (*saw*), Muslims must appoint a leader during a trip, select a leader (*imam*) to lead the prayer, and choose a leader for other group activities. In the home, the husband is the leader of his family. In the absence of her husband, the wife assumes the role of leader of the house.

In this book, we will examine what leadership is from an Islamic perspective. We will identify the characteristics of successful leaders. Islamic role models both from the *sīrah*[9] of the Prophet (*saw*) and from current history will be described in order to provide instructive examples.

Why have these leaders been so effective? A first answer is an emphasis on the locus of leadership — matching the characteristics of the leader, the follower, and the situation. A second answer relates to one of the most important roles of leaders, but one that is often neglected in Islamic organizations: the role of the leader as coach. Leaders of Islamic organizations often forget that the success of their organizations depend partly on how they recruit, train, and motivate volunteers. This topic will be discussed in detail in the coaching and delegation chapters. Another reason why some Islamic leaders are more effective than others relates to their ability to use multiple frames or perspectives across different situations. Using the same scenario, four different frames will be presented, including an integrative, Islamic frame. Finally, we will

---

[8] Reported by Abu Said al Khudri in Abu Daud, 2:721, chapter 933, hadith 2602.

[9] Biography of the Prophet Muhammad (*saw*).

describe an integrative model of leadership effectiveness in an Islamic context.

To facilitate the reader's understanding of Islamic terms, a glossary of all special terms used in this book has been added at the end of the book. In the text, these terms will be italicized.

Chapter 1
Defining Leadership

Exercise: The well-known nine-dot problem (Figure 1-1) illustrates some of the attributes of the leadership process. Connect the nine dots with four straight lines <u>without</u> lifting your pen or pencil from the paper, in one uninterrupted stroke, and without going back over the same line. The lines, however, may cross each other. What does the solution reveal about the nature of leadership?

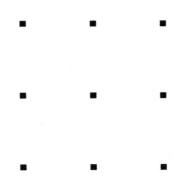

Figure 1-1: The Nine-Dot Problem

There are several solutions to this problem, but we have listed only one potential solution at the end of this chapter (p. 16). The nine dots do not, by themselves, suggest the solution space for the problem; however, almost every person trying to solve this problem will allow himself to be mentally confined by the boundaries apparently suggested by the nine dots. What does the solution suggest about leadership? As Murad indicates,[10] leadership is the ability to see beyond assumed boundaries,

---

[10] Murad, Khurram (1996). *Islamic Movement Theory and Practice: A Course for those Striving for Islamic Change in the West*. Young Muslims, UK, talk 9.

and to come up with solutions or paths that few can visualize. The leader must then project this vision for everyone to see and pursue.

An anecdote from the *sīrah* of the Prophet (*saw*) indicates his ability to envision what his companions could not. During one of the darkest times faced by the Muslims, preparing for the Battle of the Trench, he was blessed by Allah with a vision of the Ummah's future:

> After many vain attempts to split or dislodge a rock he struck, 'Umar went to the Prophet (saw) who took the pickaxe from him, and gave the rock a blow from which a spark as of lightning flashed back over the city and toward the South. He gave it another blow and again there was a flash but this time in the direction of Uhud and beyond it toward the North. A third blow split the rock into fragments, and this time the light flashed Eastward. Salman saw the three flashes and knew they must have some significance, so he asked for an interpretation from the Prophet (*saw*) who said: "Did you see them, Salman? By the light of the first, I saw the castles of Yemen; by the light of the second, I saw the castles of Syria; by the light of the third, I saw the white palace of Kisra at Mada'in. Through the first has Allah opened up to me the Yemen; through the second has He opened up to me Syria and the West, and through the third, the East.[11]

The Prophet's vision has motivated Muslims for more than a millenium. It foretold the conquering of Constantinople, for which the Muslims waited seven hundred years. Mentioning the vision still energizes Muslims to this day.

Although a leader's vision is not typically divinely inspired, it can act like a magnet as it energizes, focuses, and directs the efforts of his followers. For example, Delta Airlines' vision of becoming "the world's airline of choice" typifies the galvanizing effect that a leader can reap through a shared vision. Although Delta is not yet the best airline in the world, its employees are among the most motivated and quality-oriented in the services they provide to their customers.[12]

Vision is but one component which researchers have examined in defining leadership.[13] In this book, we will rely on two primary definitions. First, leadership is depicted as the "process by which the leader seeks the *voluntary* participation of followers in an effort to reach organizational objectives."[14]

---

[11] Lings, Martin. (1983). *Muhammad: His Life Based on the Earliest Sources*. Rochester, VT: Inner Traditions International, p. 218.

[12] Peters, T. and Waterman, R. (1982). *In Search of Excellence.* New York, NY: Warner Books.

[13] Stogdill, R. M. (1974). *Handbook of Leadership: A Survey of Theory and Research.* New York, NY: Free Press.

[14] Schriescheim, C. A., Tolliver, J. M., and Behling, O. C. (1978). "Leadership Theory: Some Implications for Managers." *MSU Topics*, Summer (26):35.

What does the above definition imply? It suggests that leadership is essentially a social exchange process. There can be no leader without followers, and no followers without a leader. The leader, as the organization's visionary, must communicate the vision with clarity and conviction. He must articulate it in terms that they can understand and relate to. The followers must share the vision and be willing to climb aboard. During this whole process, a leader will be a catalyst and a coach, a mentor, and a role model. At all times, however, a leader must remember that he cannot force others to change. They must want to change.

$$\text{لاَ إِكْرَاهَ فِى الدِّينِ قَد تَّبَيَّنَ الرُّشْدُ مِنَ الْغَيِّ فَمَن يَكْفُرْ بِالطَّٰغُوتِ وَيُؤْمِنْ بِاللَّهِ فَقَدِ اسْتَمْسَكَ بِالْعُرْوَةِ الْوُثْقَىٰ لَا انفِصَامَ لَهَا وَ اللَّهُ سَمِيعٌ عَلِيمٌ}$$

> Let there be no compulsion in religion. Truth stands out clearly from error; whoever rejects evil and believes in Allah has grasped the most trustworthy handhold that never breaks. And Allah hears and knows all things. (Baqarah, 2:256)

Allah considers the voluntary dimension of individual behavior to be so important that He emphasizes it in another verse:

$$\text{وَلَوْ شَآءَ رَبُّكَ لَآمَنَ مَن فِى الْأَرْضِ كُلُّهُمْ جَمِيعًا أَفَأَنتَ تُكْرِهُ النَّاسَ حَتَّىٰ يَكُونُواْ مُؤْمِنِينَ}$$

> If it had been the Lord's will, they would all have believed — all who are on earth! Will you then compel mankind against their will to believe! (Yunus, 10:99)

A second definition of leadership distinguishes it from the more routine processes associated with management:

> Leadership is the ability to persuade others to seek defined objectives enthusiastically. It is the human factor which binds a group together and motivates it toward goals. Management activities such as planning, organizing, and decision making are dormant cocoons until the leader

triggers the power of motivation in people and guides them toward their goals.[15]

The above definition of leadership stresses that a leader is more than just a manager. Leading and managing are not the same thing. Warren Bennis, a leadership expert, summarizes the distinction between leadership and management as follows: "The difference between managers and leaders is fundamental. The manager administers, the leader innovates. The manager maintains, the leader develops. The manager relies on systems, the leader relies on people. The manager counts on control, the leader counts on trust. The manager does things right, the leader does the right thing."[16]

An organization with good management, but poor leadership will preserve the status quo, but may not be able to advance to a higher level of performance. An organization that has an excellent leader, but nobody with good management skills may aspire to great heights, but crash precipitously because there is no one to follow through. In modern Islamic organizations, both leaders and managers are needed. Leaders can reframe experience to open new possibilities; managers can provide a sense of perspective and order so that the new possibilities become reality.

Distinguishing between Leadership, Power and Authority

Since leadership involves interpersonal influence, it is often confused with two other concepts: authority and power. Power is "the ability to marshal human, informational, and material resources to get something done,"[17] and encompasses both leadership and authority. To clarify the relationship among these concepts, we need to refer to the two primary types of power: personal and position. They can be derived from several sources or bases of a leader's power.[18] Table 1-1 summarizes these types

---

[15] Davis, K. (1967). *Human Relations at Work: The Dynamics of Organizational Behavior*. New York, NY: McGraw-Hill, p. 96.

[16] Bennis, Warren (1988). *Fortune*. January.

[17] McCall, Jr., M. (1978). Power, Influence, and Authority: The Hazards of Carrying a Sword. *Technical Report*. Greensboro, NC: Center for Creative Leadership, p. 10.

[18] French, J. R. P. and Raven, B. (1959). "The Bases of Social Power." In Dorwin Cartwright, ed. *Studies in Social Power*. Ann Arbor, Mich.: University of Michigan, pp. 150–167. Hinkin, Timothy R. and Schriescheim, Chester (1988). "Power and Influence: The View from Below." *Personnel*, May, pp. 47–50.

and bases of power. As we will see below, the Islamic perspective of leadership incorporates all seven bases of power.

Position Power

Position power is typically associated with authority, and originates from the person's position in the organization, and from four bases of power: legitimate, reward, coercive, and information.

Table 1-1: Types and Bases of Power

	Bases	Description
Position	Legitimate	The right to seek compliance by virtue of his/her position and/or delegated responsibilities.
	Reward	The ability to give recognition, promotion, pay increases, etc.
	Coercive	The use of force, including punishment, pay cuts, reprimands, etc.
	Information	The control of information others need to do their work.
Personal	Expert	Influence based on the leader's perceived knowledge and skills.
	Referent	The ability to stir willing and enthusiastic allegiance from his/her followers.
	Prestige or Reputational	The ability to get others to work by virtue of one's reputation.

1. Legitimate power

Legitimate power is associated with one's position in the organization. Generally, Islam discourages Muslims from actively seeking positions of authority. Campaigning for a position of power may imply that one is enamored with the position for one's own advancement or some other self-serving reason. 'Abdul Rahman reported the following hadith:

> The Messenger of Allah (saw) said to me: "Do not ask for a position of authority, for if you are granted this position as a result of your asking for it,

you will be left alone (without Allah's help to discharge the responsibilities involved in it), and if you are granted it without making any request for it, you will be helped (by Allah in the discharge of your duties).[19]

When can an exception be made to this injunction? When a person sees a situation in which there is a potential crisis or disaster, and he has the expertise required to help others in this situation, he may seek a specific position so as to provide assistance. In fact, the Prophet Yusuf[20] (as)[21] asked for such a position when he made the following request of the king:

$$ اجْعَلْنِى عَلَىٰ خَزَائِنِ الْأَرْضِ إِنِّى حَفِيظٌ عَلِيمٌ $$

"Set me over the storehouses of the land: I will indeed guard them as one that knows (their importance)." (Yusuf, 12: 55)

It is important to note that Ibn Kathir, in commenting upon the above verse and the action of the Prophet Yusuf (as), stresses that such a deed must be accompanied by the right intention, and must be within the parameters of Islam. Basing himself on the Qur'an,[22] Ibn Kathir concludes that:

Acceptance of righteous deeds (by Allah) depends on the fulfillment of the following two basic conditions:

- The intentions, while doing such deeds, must be totally for Allah's sake only — without any showing off or desire to gain praise or fame, etc.

- Such a deed must be performed in accordance with the Sunnah (legal ways, orders, acts of worship, statements, etc.) of Allah's Messenger, Muhammad bin 'Abdullah (saw), the last of the prophets and messengers.[23]

In fact, immediately after relating the Prophet Yusuf's (as) request, the Qur'an confirms that his intention in seeking the position of authority was indeed to serve Allah, and not self-aggrandizement:

---

[19] *Sahih Muslim*, vol. 3, page 1013.

[20] Prophet Joseph (as).

[21] *as:* upon him be peace. This is a common phrase used by Muslims whenever the name of a prophet (other than the Prophet Muhammad [saw]) is mentioned.

[22] He specifically cites Al Baqarah, 2:112.

[23] *Tafsir Ibn Kathir*, vol. 1, p. 154 as cited in *The Interpretation of the Meanings of the Noble Qur'an: A Summarized Version of Al-Tabari, Al-Qurtubi, and Ibn Kathir with Comments from Sahih al-Bukhari* (1989). Translation by Muhammad Taqi-ud Din al Hilali and Muhammad Muhsin Khan. Lahore, Pakistan: Kazi Publications, part 3, p. 234.

وَ كَذَلِكَ مَكَّنَّا لِيُوسُفَ فِى الْأَرْضِ يَتَبَوَّأُ مِنْهَا حَيْثُ يَشَآءُ نُصِيبُ بِرَحْمَتِنَا مَن نَّشَآءُ وَ لَا نُضِيعُ أَجْرَ الْمُحْسِنِينَ

> Thus did We give established power to Yusuf in the land to take possession therein as when or where he pleased. We bestow of Our mercy on whom We please and We suffer not to be lost the reward of those who do good. (Yusuf, 12:56)

2. Reward power

A leader who has position power may also control organizational rewards, including pay raises, desirable work assignments, or vacation breaks. It is noteworthy that 'Umar ibn al Khattab[24] (ra)[25] used to pay state officials high salaries. He wanted to ensure that they would not be tempted by bribes. By treating his appointees equitably, 'Umar (ra) became one of the most outstanding Islamic leaders. At the same time, misuse of the reward system by the leader can lead to corruption and decay. .'Umar (ra) understood this perfectly, and wanted to prevent any Muslim leader appointed by him from misusing reward power. This is partly why he removed Khalid ibn Walid (ra), one of the most brilliant strategists and military leaders in the history of Islam, from command:

> Khalid ibn Walid (ra) was a successful and powerful general of Islam. He occupies a unique position in the history of heroism. He devoted his whole life to the cause of Islam. 'Umar (ra) always appreciated his services. But there were certain complaints against him, especially for being extravagant, [for example,] when he awarded 10,000 dinars to a poet. Khalid could not give a satisfactory explanation to 'Umar (ra), hence, he was removed from the command. But Khalid proved to be a very true Muslim and fought like an ordinary soldier in the army ... [He] was deposed when the battle of Yarmuk was going on. The Caliph's order was delivered to Khalid but it had no effect on him. He went on fighting as fiercely as before. After the battle was over, his dismissal became known. When somebody asked him why the news did not dampen his spirit at all, he said, "I was fighting for the cause of Allah."[26]

---

[24] Second caliph in Islam. Unless otherwise noted, 'Umar ibn al Khattab (ra) will be referred to as 'Umar.

[25] *Radi Allahu anhu (ra):* May Allah be pleased with him. Mentioned after the name of a companion of the Prophet. See Glossary.

[26] Par Excellence Computers (1996). Prominent Muslims, *Islamic Scholar.* South Africa: Johannesburg.

It is important to note that Khalid (*ra*) did not think that he had abused his power. 'Umar, however, perceived a faint pattern of potential abuse, and did not want to run the risk that Khalid might take advantage of his position one day.

3. Coercive power

Besides controlling organizational rewards, a leader in a position of authority also controls group sanctions. For example, after several warnings, the leader may reprimand an individual who is consistently producing poor quality work. He or she may withhold a bonus from an employee who always comes to work late. Islam recognizes the legitimacy of coercive power; at the same time, it makes explicit the conditions under which followers can rise against the use of coercive power by a leader. The following hadith narrated by 'Ali ibn Abu Talib[27] (*ra*) illustrates the safeguards placed by Islam against the abuse of coercive power:

> The Prophet sent an army unit (for some campaign) and appointed a man from the Ansar as its commander and ordered them (the soldiers) to obey him. (During the campaign) he became angry with them and said, "Didn't the Prophet order you to obey me?" They said, "Yes." He said, "I order you to collect wood and make a fire and then throw yourselves into it." So they collected wood and made a fire, but when they were about to throw themselves into it, they started looking at each other. Some of them said, "We followed the Prophet to escape from the fire. How should we enter it now?" So while they were in that state, the fire extinguished and their commander's anger abated. The event was mentioned to the Prophet and he said, "If they had entered it (the fire) they would never have come out of it, for obedience is required only in what is good."[28]

Hence, a leader must be careful when using coercive power. Its use, during anger, can easily lead to abuses. Under no condition can an amir give a command which, as in the case above, is contrary to a clear Islamic injunction.

4. Information power

People need information to do their work. To the extent that a leader has access to or controls this information, he is likely to receive a lot of cooperation from his followers.

---

[27] Fourth caliph of Islam. Unless otherwise noted, 'Ali ibn Abu Talib (*ra*) will be referred to as 'Ali.

[28] *Sahih Bukhari*, volume 9, hadith 259. See also *Sahih Bukhari*, volume 5, hadith 629.

Personal Power

Personal power derives from the person rather than from the organization or position he occupies. Three bases are associated with personal power: expert power, referent power, and prestige or reputational power.

1. Expert power

Leaders who possess valuable expertise and information have expert power with respect to their followers who need this information to perform their task. For example, brothers or sisters with expertise in hardware or software are in great demand in Islamic organizations, and exercise a great deal of expert power over others who are less knowledgeable or nontechnical. In a prayer congregation, expert power in Islam and the Islamic Shar'iah is one of the reasons why somebody is chosen to lead the prayers. This aspect of power will be discussed in further detail in the chapter dealing with the locus of leadership.

2. Referent or charismatic power

A person has charisma when others wish to follow him because they are attracted by his personality. Born leaders are usually charismatic. There are two types of charismatic leaders: *Ethical charismatic leaders*, such as the Prophet (*saw*) and all other prophets (*as*), who use power for the benefit of mankind, learn from criticism, work to develop their followers into leaders, and rely on an internal moral standard; and *unethical charismatic leaders,* who are motivated by self-interest, who censure critical or opposing views, and who lack an internal moral code (e.g., Stalin and Hitler).

The Prophet Muhammad (*saw*) had a very charismatic personality. Urwa Bin Masud was sent by the Quraish at the time of Hudaibiyah to the Prophet (*saw*) to settle the situation with him. When he returned, he said, "I have been to Chosroes in his kingdom, Caesar in his kingdom, and the Negus in his kingdom, but never have I seen a king among a people like Muhammad among his companions. I have seen a people who will never abandon him for any reason; so form your own opinion."[29]

In the United States, a very charismatic Muslim leader was Malcolm X. Many embraced Islam after listening to or reading about, him.

---

[29] Ibn Ishaq, p. 503, as reported by Rahman, Afzalur (1990) in *Muhammad as a Military Leader*. Lahore, Pakistan: Islamic Publications, p. 67.

[Malcolm X's] life showed me something eminently more useful than skilled oratory: What role religion could play as one approached this race-conscious society. He provided an example of how a man could use conviction as a powerful instrument to change the course of life — one's own and others. His remarkable ability to transform himself from hood to cleaned-up spokesman for the Nation of Islam and then for Sunni Islam — that was the real message.[30]

3. Prestige or reputational power

A leader who has a track record of success acquires prestige or reputational power. This type of power has been clearly exhibited by the Prophet (saw) on several occasions. Listen to him speaking to his people from the mount of Al Safa:

"Tell me, O men of Quraysh, if I were to inform you that I see a cavalry on the other side of this mountain, would you believe me?" They answered: "Indeed, for we trust you and have never known you to tell a lie." Muhammad (saw) said: "Know then that I am a warner, and that I warn you of a severe punishment." [31]

When we consider the above description of the two types of power, we see that the more a leader accesses both power of person and position, the more effective he will be. Overall, a leader who has authority but less expertise than other organizational members is much less effective than a leader who has access to both bases of power. By contrast, a leader with charismatic power but little authority will find himself or herself clashing constantly with the chain of command. In placing brothers or sisters in leadership positions, organizational designers need to remember that access to multiple bases of power may be necessary for these leaders to fulfill their role as expected. Exercising multiple types of power does not by itself guarantee that a leader will be effective. He or she will also need to understand the roles that the leader is to play.

Leadership Roles from an Islamic Perspective

According to Islam, the two primary roles of a leader are those of servant-leader and guardian-leader.

---

[30] Barboza, S. (1994). *American Jihad: Islam after Malcolm X*. New York, NY: Doubleday, p. 16.

[31] Haykal, M. H. (1976). *The Life of Muhammad (saw)*. Indianapolis, IN: American Trust Publications, p. 85.

Servant-leader

Leaders are servants of their followers (*sayyid al qawn khadimuhum*).[32] They seek their welfare and guide them toward what is good. The Prophet (*saw*) said:

> A ruler who has been entrusted with the affairs of the Muslims, but makes no endeavor (for their material and moral upliftment) and is not sincerely concerned (for their welfare) will not enter Paradise along with them.[33]

The idea of a leader as a servant has been part of Islam since its beginning, and has only recently been developed by Robert Greenleaf:[34]

> The servant-leader is servant first ... It begins with the natural feeling that one wants to serve, to serve *first*. ... The best test, and the most difficult to administer, is: Do those served grow as persons? Do they, *while being served*, become healthier, wiser, freer, more autonomous, more likely themselves to become servants? *And,* what is the effect on the least privileged in society; will they benefit or, at least, not be further deprived?

Guardian-leader

The example of the Prophet Muhammad (*saw*) emphasizes a second major role of the Muslim leader: to protect his community against tyranny and oppression, to encourage Allah-consciousness and *taqwa*, and to promote justice.

> All of you are guardians and are responsible for your wards. The ruler is a guardian and the man is a guardian of his family; the lady is a guardian and is responsible for her husband's house and his offspring; and so all of you are guardians and are responsible for your wards.[35]

Further it is reported from Abu Hurairah:

> The Prophet of Allah (peace be upon him) said, "A commander (of the Muslims) is a shield for them. They fight behind him and they are protected by him (from tyrants and aggressors). If he enjoins fear of Allah, the Exalted and Glorious, and dispenses justice, there will be a (great) reward for him; and if he enjoins otherwise, it redounds on him."[36]

---

[32] Kasule, Sr., Omar Hassan (1998). "Leadership Module. General Theme: Leadership. Workshop 1." In *Muslim Leaders' Forum 98 Handbook.* Kuala Lumpur, Malaysia: Tarbiyyah and Training Center, International Islamic University Malaysia, p. 3.

[33] Reported by Abu Malih in *Sahih Muslim* 1:82, Chapter 44, Hadith no. 264.

[34] Greenleaf, Robert. (1970). *The Servant as Leader.* Indianapolis, IN: Greenleaf Center for Servant-Leadership, p. 7.

[35] Reported by Ibn 'Umar, *Sahih Bukhari*, 7.128.

[36] Abu Hurairah, in *Sahih Muslim*, hadith no. 4542.

Solution to the Nine-dot Problem

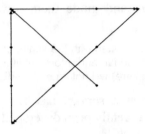

Figure 1-2: Solution to the 9-Dot Problem

Chapter 2
The Moral Bases of Islamic Leadership

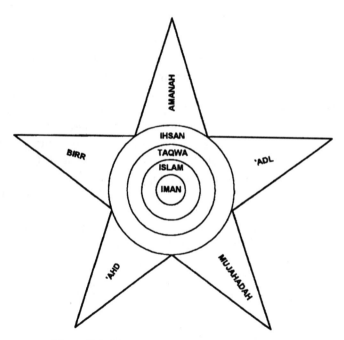

Figure 2-1: Moral Bases of Islamic Leadership

Moral Bases of Islamic Leadership

Leadership in Islam is rooted in belief and willing submission to the Creator, Allah. It centers on serving Him. The primary tasks of leaders

are to do good deeds and to work toward the establishment of Allah's
dīn.[37]

وَ جَعَلْنٰهُمْ أَئِمَّةً يَهْدُونَ بِأَمْرِنا وَ أَوْحَيْنَآ إِلَيْهِمْ فِعْلَ

الْخَيْرٰتِ وَإِقَامَ الصَّلٰوةِ وَإِيْتَآءَ الزَّكٰوةِ وَكَانُوا لَنَا

عٰبِدِينَ

> And We made them leaders guiding (men) by Our
> command and We sent them inspiration to do good
> deeds, to establish regular prayers and to practice
> regular charity; and they constantly served Us (and
> Us only). (Anbiyaa, 21:73)

With reference to the above verse, let us note that the good deeds of the
leader must be preceded by good intentions; otherwise, a leader may
intend harm, but end up performing good deeds fortuitously. Good
deeds preceded by evil intentions are not meritorious. Further, the
establishment of Islam is to be done *without* coercing anyone into
becoming a Muslim against his or her will (see Baqarah, 2:256).

Very few Muslim leaders have understood and put into practice the
above divine injunction as well as 'Umar ibn al Khattab (*ra*) did. The
paradigm of leadership 'Umar (*ra*) adopted led to a governance structure
centered on Islamic teachings. This structure was critical in cementing
together the vast Islamic lands that he oversaw. An example of 'Umar's
(*ra*) strength of belief can be easily ascertained in the instructions he
gave to Sa'd bin Abi Waqqas (*ra*) as the latter was leaving with the
Muslim army to face the Persian Empire before the Battle of Qadisiya:

> Allah does not repel evil with evil but he repels evil with good. All men high
> and low are equal before Him. One can win Allah's favor only through
> devotion to His service. Remember that the Sunnah (the Way) of the Holy
> Prophet is the only correct way of doing things. You are going on a heavy
> mission which you can discharge only by following the Truth. Inculcate good
> habits in yourselves and in your companions.[38]

'Umar's (*ra*) depth of *iman* and strength of character are why the
Prophet (*saw*) gave 'Umar the title "Al Faruq," — the one who makes a
distinction between Truth (*haqq*) and falsehood (*batil*).

---

[37] *Dīn* is the way of living ordained by Allah.

[38] *Islamic Scholar*, Prominent Muslims.

To follow the example of 'Umar, a Muslim leader needs to act in accordance with the injunction of Allah and His Prophet (*saw*), and must develop a strong Islamic moral character. This moral character will be reflected by his *yaqin* (conviction):

$$\text{وَجَعَلْنَا مِنْهُمْ أَئِمَّةً يَهْدُونَ بِأَمْرِنَا لَمَّا صَبَرُوا وَكَانُوا}$$

$$\text{بِآيَاتِنَا يُوقِنُونَ}$$

> And We appointed from among them leaders giving guidance under Our command so long as they persevered with patience and continued to have faith in Our signs. (Sajdah, 32:24)

The more turbulent the environment in which the leader functions, the more unshakeable his/her conviction must be. Often, leaders have to endure tremendous hardships: vilification, prison, exile, harsh words, and in some cases execution. For example, Maudoodi, Syed Qutb, and Muhammad Ali all experienced prison terms and the wrath of the media. Syed Qutb was executed because of what he embodied, and Maudoodi faced hanging. A deep conviction coupled with patience (which will be discussed in a later chapter) is essential if a leader wants to challenge the status quo and reform a society or an organization. The source of a leader's conviction in Allah's signs (*yaqin*) is his faith in Allah or *iman*.

Iman

We have depicted the bases of Islamic moral character[39] in Figure 2-1, and will discuss their implications with respect to the leader-follower relationship in this chapter. In a hadith narrated by 'Abdullah ibn 'Umar ibn al Khattab, the Prophet states the following about *iman*:

> [It is] that you affirm your faith in Allah, in His angels, in His books, in His messengers, in the Day of Judgment, and you affirm your faith in the Divine Decree about good and evil.[40]

At the core of Islamic moral character is *iman* or faith in Allah. *Iman* implies belief in the Oneness of Allah (*tawhid*) and the prophethood of Muhammad (*saw*). An individual with strong *iman* will consider himself and all his possessions as belonging to Allah. He will bow his ego, his

---

[39] Maudoodi, Sayyid, Abu A'la. *The Islamic Movement: Dynamics of Values, Power and Change.* Edited by Khurram Murad (1991). Leicester, UK: The Islamic Foundation.

[40] 'Abdullah ibn 'Umar ibn al Khattab, *Sahih Muslim*, hadith 1.

ideas, his passions, and his thinking before Allah. He will obey the injunctions of Allah (*hudud*) and His Prophet without hesitation.

وَمَا كَانَ لِمُؤْمِنٍ وَلاَ مُؤْمِنَةٍ إِذَا قَضَى اللَّهُ وَرَسُولُهُ

أَمْرًا أَن يَكُونَ لَهُمُ الْخِيَرَةُ مِنْ أَمْرِهِمْ وَمَن يَعْصِ اللَّهَ

وَرَسُولَهُ فَقَدْ ضَلَّ ضَلَالاً مُّبِينًا

> It is not fitting for a believer, man or woman, when a matter has been decided by Allah and His Messenger to have any option about their decision: if anyone disobeys Allah and His Messenger he is indeed on a clearly wrong Path. (Al Ahzab, 33:36)

Iman also implies belief in the *akhirah* (the next life), and in one's ultimate accountability for one's deeds. A leader with firm *iman* will not dodge responsibility for his actions, and will be cautious about any directives that he gives to his followers. He will continuously emphasize good deeds. To reinforce this idea, the Qur'an links *iman* with good deeds — *'amal salih* — no less than sixty times.

Although it is highly desirable to look for a leader with *iman*, it may not always be possible to find someone who has the requisite skills and is at the same time a strong Muslim. An Islamic organization may have to choose between a strong Muslim with weak leadership skills or a strong leader with moderate or weak Islamic understanding. The example of Amr ibn al 'Aas is to be remembered here. He had been a Muslim for only four months when he was appointed by the Prophet (*saw*) to lead the Muslims at the battle of Dhat al Salasil. This issue was explained by Ibn Taymiyya in his book *Assiyasah Ash-Shar'iyya*.[41] A leader with weak or inadequate expertise can bring disaster to an organization whereas a skilled leader may advance and help the same organization. Even if the skilled leader is deficient in Islamic practice, his shortcomings can be made up through the *shura* process of decision making. Altough less knowledgeable in certain areas, the leader must be willing and able to accept guidance from others in these and other areas. Otherwise, he may lead his followers astray.

---

[41] Jabnoun, Naceur. (1994) *Islam and Management*. Kuala Lumpur, Malaysia: Institut Kajian Dasar (IKD).

Islam

Building upon *iman*, *Islam* is the second layer of the moral personality of an Islamic leader and followers. The term "Islam" comes from the Arabic root "SLM" which means peace and submission. Islam means the achievement of peace with Allah, within oneself and with the creation of Allah, through willing submission to Him. The Prophet Muhammad (*saw*) has defined what *Islam* is:

> Islam implies that you testify that there is no god but Allah and that Muhammad is the messenger of Allah, and you establish prayer, pay Zakat, observe the fast of Ramadan, and perform pilgrimage to the (House) if you are solvent enough (to bear the expense of) the journey.[42]

As Maudoodi points out so well, "*Iman* is the seed and *Islam* is the fruition."[43] Because of his or her *iman*, an individual's life will be conducted according to Islamic principles. Conversely, if an individual behaves un-Islamically, his *iman* may be nonexistent or very weak. Inner faith and practice are tightly coupled with one another and are interdependent. A leader who practices Islam will submit his ego to Allah, and will never see himself as supreme. 'Ali ibn Abu Talib's (*ra*) letter to Malik al Ashtar al Nakha'i, the new Governor of Egypt, stresses this point in the following manner:

> Malik, you must never forget that if you are a ruler over them, then the Caliph is a ruler over you, and Allah is the supreme Lord over the Caliph.[44]

Sovereignty, then, belongs to Allah only, and any leader who becomes overly arrogant or any follower who idolizes his or her leader needs to remember the story of Pharaoh in the Qur'an.

$$\text{وَ لَقَدْ أَرْسَلْنَا مُوسَىٰ بِآيَاتِنَا وَ سُلْطَانٍ مُّبِينٍ}$$

$$\text{إِلَىٰ فِرْعَوْنَ وَمَلَإِيْهِ فَاتَّبَعُوا أَمْرَ فِرْعَوْنَ وَمَا أَمْرُ}$$

$$\text{فِرْعَوْنَ بِرَشِيدٍ}$$

$$\text{يَقْدُمُ قَوْمَهُ يَوْمَ الْقِيَامَةِ فَأَوْرَدَهُمُ النَّارَ وَبِئْسَ الْوِرْدُ}$$

$$\text{الْمَوْرُودُ}$$

---

[42] 'Abdullah ibn 'Umar ibn al Khattab, *Sahih Muslim*, hadith 1.

[43] Maudoodi, p. 115.

[44] Behzadnia, A. A. and Denny, S. *To the Commander in Chief from Imam 'Ali to Malik al Ashter* (circa 1980), p. 8.

And We sent Moses with Our clear (signs) and an
authority manifest unto Pharaoh and his chiefs: but
they followed the command of Pharaoh and the
command of Pharaoh was not rightly guided. He
will go before his people on the Day of Judgment
and lead them into the Fire (as cattle are led to
water): but woeful indeed will be this leading (and)
the place led to! (Hud, 11:96–98).

Taqwa

As an individual submits to Allah through Islam, he or she develops an
awe of Allah. *Taqwa* is the all-encompassing, inner consciousness of
one's duty toward Him and the awareness of one's accountability toward
Him.[45] As pointed out by Maudoodi, "The essence of *taqwa* lies in an
attitude of heart and mind rather than in an outward form."[46] When
imbued with *taqwa*, a person's frame of mind — his thoughts, emotions
and inclinations — will reflect Islam. His awe and fear of Allah will
lead him to be proactive, and avoid any behavior that may be outside the
limits prescribed by Allah. Those who have *taqwa* are described as those
who believe in the Qur'an:

$$ذَٰلِكَ ٱلْكِتَـٰبُ لَارَيْبَ ۛ فِيهِ ۛ هُدًى لِّلْمُتَّقِينَ$$

$$ٱلَّذِينَ يُؤْمِنُونَ بِٱلْغَيْبِ وَ يُقِيمُونَ ٱلصَّلَوٰةَ وَمِمَّا رَزَقْنَـٰهُمْ يُنفِقُونَ$$

$$وَ ٱلَّذِينَ يُؤْمِنُونَ بِمَآ أُنزِلَ إِلَيْكَ وَمَآ أُنزِلَ مِن قَبْلِكَ وَبِٱلْـَٔاخِرَةِ هُمْ يُوقِنُونَ$$

$$أُو۟لَـٰٓئِكَ عَلَىٰ هُدًى مِّن رَّبِّهِمْ وَأُو۟لَـٰٓئِكَ هُمُ ٱلْمُفْلِحُونَ$$

This is the Book; in it is guidance sure without
doubt to those who fear Allah *(muttaqin)*, who
believe in the unseen, are steadfast in prayer and
spend out of what We have provided for them, and
who believe in the Revelation sent to you and sent

[45] Ibid., p. 116.
[46] Ibid., p. 118.

before your time and (in their hearts) have the
assurance of the Hereafter. They are on (true)
guidance from their Lord and it is these who will
prosper. (Al Baqarah, 2:2–5)

Taqwa restrains a Muslim leader or follower from behaving un-
Islamically — whether to community members, to customers, to
suppliers, or to anybody else.

إِنَّ اللَّهَ يَأْمُرُ بِالْعَدْلِ وَالْإِحْسَـٰنِ وَ إِيتَآىِٕ ذِى الْقُرْبَىٰ
وَيَنْهَىٰ عَنِ الْفَحْشَآءِ وَالْمُنْكَرِ وَالْبَغْىِ يَعِظُكُمْ لَعَلَّكُمْ
تَذَكَّرُونَ

Allah commands justice, the doing of good, and
liberality to kith and kin; and He forbids all
shameful deeds, injustice, and rebellion: He
instructs you that you may receive admonition.
(Nahl, 16:90)

The behavior of the *muttaqin* (those who have *taqwa*) is described
further in the following verse:

لَيْسَ ٱلْبِرَّ أَن تُوَلُّوا۟ وُجُوهَكُمْ قِبَلَ ٱلْمَشْرِقِ وَ ٱلْمَغْرِبِ
وَلَٰكِنَّ ٱلْبِرَّ مَنْ ءَامَنَ بِٱللَّهِ وَٱلْيَوْمِ ٱلْآخِرِ وَ ٱلْمَلَـٰٓئِكَةِ
وَٱلْكِتَـٰبِ وَ ٱلنَّبِيِّـۧنَ وَ ءَاتَى ٱلْمَالَ عَلَىٰ حُبِّهِ ذَوِى
ٱلْقُرْبَىٰ وَٱلْيَتَـٰمَىٰ وَ ٱلْمَسَـٰكِينَ وَٱبْنَ ٱلسَّبِيلِ وَ
ٱلسَّآئِلِينَ وَفِى ٱلرِّقَابِ وَ أَقَامَ ٱلصَّلَـٰوةَ وَءَاتَى ٱلزَّكَوٰةَ وَ
ٱلْمُوفُونَ بِعَهْدِهِمْ إِذَا عَـٰهَدُوا۟ وَ ٱلصَّـٰبِرِينَ فِى ٱلْبَأْسَآءِ وَ
ٱلضَّرَّآءِ وَحِينَ ٱلْبَأْسِ أُو۟لَـٰٓئِكَ ٱلَّذِينَ صَدَقُوا۟ وَأُو۟لَـٰٓئِكَ
هُمُ ٱلْمُتَّقُونَ

> It is not righteousness that you turn your faces
> toward the East or West; but it is righteousness to
> believe in Allah, the Last Day, the angels, the Book,
> and the messengers; to spend of your substance out
> of love for Him for your kin, for orphans, for the
> needy, for the wayfarer, for those who ask, and for
> the ransom of slaves; to be steadfast in prayer and
> practice regular charity; to fulfil the contracts which
> you have made; and to be firm and patient in pain
> (or suffering), adversity, and throughout all periods
> of panic. Such are the people of truth, the God-
> fearing *(muttaqin)*. (Al Baqarah, 2:177)

Based on the above verses, several moral attributes of the *muttaqin* that
apply to the behavior of Muslim leaders and followers are salient:

- They act justly, and do not not allow their personal feelings to
  hamper justice.
- They take care of those in need, and do so for the love of Allah.
- They are steadfast in prayer and practice charity.
- They observe all contracts and do not break their word.
- They are patient and firm, no matter what adversity or personal
  suffering they may be experiencing.

These general attributes of leaders and followers will be discussed in
detail in Chapter 3.

Ihsan

Whereas *taqwa* is the fear of Allah and the feeling of Allah's presence,
ihsan is the love of Allah. This love of Allah motivates the individual
Muslim to work toward attaining Allah's pleasure. In a hadith reported
by Abu Huraira,[47] the Prophet Muhammad *(saw)* describes *ihsan* as
follows: "To worship Allah as if you see Him, and if you cannot achieve
this state of devotion, then you must consider that He is looking at you."
The constant feeling that Allah is watching is likely to prompt a person
with *Ihsan* to behave at his best. The difference between the *muttaqin*
(Muslims with *taqwa*) and the *Muhsinin* (Muslims with *ihsan*) is
explained concisely by Maudoodi in the following example.[48] Among
government employees, there may be some who perform their duties
scrupulously, but who do not demonstrate any additional commitment.
Other employees, however, push themselves beyond the call of duty;

---

[47] *Sahih Bukhari*, 1: 47.
[48] Ibid., p. 119.

they are energized, and willing to make sacrifices in the performance of their tasks. They spare no effort to support their government, and champion its cause without holding back. Within the context of Islam, the first group of employees are like believers who do what is sufficient and necessary; they are the *muttaqin*. By contrast, the second group of employees can be compared to the *muhsinin*. These are the Muslim leaders and followers who will tirelessly carry the banner of Islam under the most difficult circumstances. This is why Allah has reserved tremendous rewards for the *muhsinin*.

وَكَأَيِّن مِّن نَّبِيٍّ قَٰتَلَ مَعَهُ رِبِّيُّونَ كَثِيرٌ فَمَا وَهَنُوا

لِمَآ أَصَابَهُمْ فِى سَبِيلِ ٱللَّهِ وَمَا ضَعُفُوا وَمَا ٱسْتَكَانُوا

وَٱللَّهُ يُحِبُّ ٱلصَّٰبِرِينَ

وَمَا كَانَ قَوْلَهُمْ إِلَّا أَن قَالُوا رَبَّنَا ٱغْفِرْ لَنَا

ذُنُوبَنَا وَإِسْرَافَنَا فِىٓ أَمْرِنَا وَثَبِّتْ أَقْدَامَنَا وَٱنصُرْنَا

عَلَى ٱلْقَوْمِ ٱلْكَٰفِرِينَ

فَـَٔاتَٰهُمُ ٱللَّهُ ثَوَابَ ٱلدُّنْيَا وَحُسْنَ ثَوَابِ ٱلْـَٔاخِرَةِ وَٱللَّهُ

يُحِبُّ ٱلْمُحْسِنِينَ

> How many of the prophets fought (in Allah's way) and with them (fought) large bands of Godly men? But they never lost heart if they met with disaster in Allah's way nor did they weaken (in will) nor give in. And Allah loves those who are firm and steadfast. All that they said was: "Our Lord! forgive us our sins and anything we may have done that transgressed our duty; establish our feet firmly and help us against those that resist faith." And Allah gave them a reward in this world and the excellent reward of the Hereafter. For Allah loves the *muhsinin*. (Al 'Imran, 3:146–8)

Based on the above discussion of the four layers of Islamic moral character, leaders and followers may be classified acording to their stage: *iman*, *Islam*, *taqwa* and *ihsan*. Depending on their stage, they can be

expected to emphasize the following five key parameters of Islamic
behavior:

1. *'Adl* or justice and equity.[49] Justice is a dynamic characteristic that
   each Muslim must strive to develop whether he is a leader or a
   follower.

$$يَـٰٓأَيُّهَا ٱلَّذِينَ ءَامَنُواْ كُونُواْ قَوَّٰمِينَ لِلَّهِ شُهَدَآءَ$$

$$بِٱلْقِسْطِ وَ لَا يَجْرِمَنَّكُمْ شَنَـٔانُ قَوْمٍ عَلَىٰٓ أَلَّا تَعْدِلُواْ$$

$$ٱعْدِلُواْ هُوَ أَقْرَبُ لِلتَّقْوَىٰ وَٱتَّقُواْ ٱللَّهَ إِنَّ ٱللَّهَ خَبِيرٌۢ بِمَا$$

$$تَعْمَلُونَ$$

> O you who believe! Stand out firmly for Allah as
> witnesses to fair dealing and let not the hatred of
> others to you make you swerve to wrong and depart
> from justice. Be just: that is next to piety: and fear
> Allah for Allah is well-acquainted with all that you
> do. (Al Maida, 5:8)

The term *'adl* can mean either justice or balance. The need to achieve
a balance and to take a middle road is quite important in a leader, and
is stressed repeatedly by Allah in the Qur'an. He describes "those who
will be rewarded with the highest place in heaven" as:

$$وَ ٱلَّذِينَ إِذَآ أَنفَقُواْ لَمْ يُسْرِفُواْ وَ لَمْ يَقْتُرُواْ وَكَانَ$$

$$بَيْنَ ذَٰلِكَ قَوَامًا$$

$$وَ ٱلَّذِينَ لَا يَدْعُونَ مَعَ ٱللَّهِ إِلَـٰهًا ءَاخَرَ وَلَا يَقْتُلُونَ$$

$$ٱلنَّفْسَ ٱلَّتِى حَرَّمَ ٱللَّهُ إِلَّا بِٱلْحَقِّ وَلَا يَزْنُونَ وَمَن يَفْعَلْ$$

$$ذَٰلِكَ يَلْقَ أَثَامًا$$

---

[49] Umar-ud-din (1991), Muhammad. *The Ethical Philosophy of Al-Ghazzali*. Lahore,
Pakistan: Sh. Muhammad Ashraf, p. 241.

وَ الَّذِينَ لَا يَشْهَدُونَ الزُّورَ وَإِذَا مَرُّوا بِاللَّغْوِ مَرُّوا كِرَامًا

وَ الَّذِينَ إِذَا ذُكِّرُوا بِآيَاتِ رَبِّهِمْ لَمْ يَخِرُّوا عَلَيْهَا صُمًّا

وَعُمْيَانًا

> Those who, when they spend, are not extravagant
> and not niggardly, but hold a just (balance) between
> those two extremes; those who invoke not with
> Allah, any other god ... those who witness no
> falsehood and, if they pass by futility, they pass by
> it with honorable (avoidance); those who, when they
> are admonished with the signs of their Lord, droop
> not down at them as if they were deaf or blind.
> (Furqan, 25: 67–68, 72–73)

Application of 'adl to leadership. The principle of justice must be
observed by all Muslims — leaders and followers alike. For example,
Allah admonishes Muslims thus:

إِنَّ اللَّهَ يَأْمُرُكُمْ أَن تُؤَدُّوا الْأَمَانَاتِ إِلَىٰ أَهْلِهَا وَإِذَا

حَكَمْتُم بَيْنَ النَّاسِ أَن تَحْكُمُوا بِالْعَدْلِ ۚ إِنَّ اللَّهَ نِعِمَّا

يَعِظُكُم بِهِ ۗ إِنَّ اللَّهَ كَانَ سَمِيعًا بَصِيرًا

> Allah commands you to render back your trusts to
> those to whom they are due; and when you judge
> between man and man that you judge with justice:
> verily how excellent is the teaching which He gives
> you! for Allah is He who hears and sees all things.
> (Al Nisaa, 4:58)

This is why the Prophet (*saw*) emphasized that justice must never be
compromised by personal affiliations or other considerations. The
following example illustrates how seriously Muslim leaders and
followers should view justice:

A lady committed theft during the lifetime of Allah's Messenger in the
ghazwa of *Al Fath* (i.e., conquest of Makkah). Her folk went to Usama bin
Zaid to intercede for her (with the Prophet). When Usama interceded for her
with Allah's Messenger, the color of the face of Allah's Messenger changed
and he said, "Do you intercede with me in a matter involving one of the legal
punishments prescribed by Allah?" Usama said, "O Allah's Messenger! Ask

Allah's forgiveness for me." So in the afternoon, Allah's Messenger got up
and addressed the people. He praised Allah as He deserved and then said,
"*Amma ba'du!* The nations prior to you were destroyed because if a noble
among them stole, they used to excuse him, and if a poor person amongst
them stole, they would apply (Allah's) legal punishment to him."[50]

Notwithstanding her lineage, the lady was punished appropriately, and
she later repented.

2. *Amānah* or trust.   This concept stresses the idea of responsibility
    toward organizational stakeholders, and holds true whether those
    entrusting something to Muslims are themselves non-Muslims.

$$\text{يَـٰٓأَيُّهَا ٱلَّذِينَ ءَامَنُواْ لَا تَخُونُواْ ٱللَّهَ وَ ٱلرَّسُولَ وَتَخُونُوٓاْ}$$

$$\text{أَمَـٰنَـٰتِكُمْ وَأَنتُمْ تَعْلَمُونَ}$$

> O you who believe! betray not the trust of Allah and
> the Messenger nor misappropriate knowingly things
> entrusted to you. (Anfaal, 8:27)

As a core value, *amānah* fits within an overall Islamic etiquette
governing social relationships. 'Ubadah Ibn al Samit, reported that:

The Prophet (saw) said, "If you guarantee me six things on your part I shall
guarantee you Paradise. Speak the truth when you talk, keep a promise
when you make it, when you are entrusted with something fulfill your trust,
avoid sexual immorality, lower your eyes, and restrain your hands from
injustice." Ahmad and Bayhaqi, in *Shu'ab al Iman* transmitted it.[51]

Application of *amānah* to leadership. The Qur'an explicitly links the
concept of *amānah* to leadership.   We refer to the story of Prophet
Yusuf (*as*):

$$\text{وَ قَالَ الْمَلِكُ ائْتُونِي بِهِ أَسْتَخْلِصْهُ لِنَفْسِي فَلَمَّا}$$

$$\text{كَلَّمَهُ قَالَ إِنَّكَ الْيَوْمَ لَدَيْنَا مَكِينٌ أَمِينٌ}$$

$$\text{قَالَ اجْعَلْنِي عَلَىٰ خَزَائِنِ الْأَرْضِ إِنِّي حَفِيظٌ عَلِيمٌ}$$

---

[50] *Sahih al Bukhari*, hadith 5.597.
[51] "Mishkat al Masabih," in *Islamic Scholar* (1996). Johannesburg, South Africa, 4870.

> So the king said: "Bring him to me; I will take him
> specially to serve about my own person." Therefore
> when he had spoken to him he said: "Be assured this
> day you are before our own Presence with rank
> firmly established and fidelity fully proved!"
> (Yusuf) said: "Set me over the storehouses of the
> land: I will indeed guard them as one that knows
> (their importance)." (Yusuf, 12:54–55)

After the king had indicated that he placed great trust in him, the
Prophet Yusuf (*as*) deliberately asked to be put in charge of the
granaries and storehouses, and the demanding task of establishing
them and guarding them. As one translator of the Qur'an, 'Abdullah
Yusuf Ali, points out, the Prophet Yusuf (*as*) understood the need to
build reserves better than anyone else, and was prepared to take on this
task himself rather than burden another with the task of restricting
supplies in times of plenty.[52] He had the necessary expertise, and
backed by the king's trust, he felt that he could, *insha' Allah*,
effectively perform this difficult task.

Once an individual has accepted to be the leader of a group or
organization, he has in fact accepted a trust. His behavior should
conform to what the Prophet (*saw*) described in the hadith just cited
above: speak the truth; keep one's promise; fulfill one's trust; avoid
sexual transgressions, practice modesty and behave justly. In all
Islamic organizations, a leader is entrusted with the responsibility of
making strategic, long-term decisions for the community. In a for-
profit, Muslim organization, the management of the organization is
entrusted with the shareholders' investment. In a nonprofit
organization, the management of the organization is charged with
watching over the properties of the trust (*waqf*). Consequently, any
managerial decision must be balanced with respect for this trust. The
concept of *amānah* can be extended to other dimensions of one's work
as a leader or a follower. Should one be wasting time or
organizational resources in performing one's task, one is violating
one's *amānah*.

3. **Birr** or righteousness. Righteous behavior is described in the
following verse:

---

[52] Abdullah Yusuf Ali. (1989). *The Holy Qur'an: Text, Translation and Commentary.*
Beltsville, MD: Amana Publications, comment 1716.

لَيْسَ ٱلْبِرَّ أَن تُوَلُّواْ وُجُوهَكُمْ قِبَلَ ٱلْمَشْرِقِ وَ ٱلْمَغْرِبِ

وَلَـٰكِنَّ ٱلْبِرَّ مَنْ ءَامَنَ بِٱللَّهِ وَٱلْيَوْمِ ٱلْأَخِرِ وَ ٱلْمَلَـٰئِكَةِ

وَٱلْكِتَـٰبِ وَ ٱلنَّبِيِّـۧنَ وَ ءَاتَى ٱلْمَالَ عَلَىٰ حُبِّهِ ذَوِى

ٱلْقُرْبَىٰ وَٱلْيَتَـٰمَىٰ وَ ٱلْمَسَـٰكِينَ وَٱبْنَ ٱلسَّبِيلِ وَ

ٱلسَّآئِلِينَ وَفِى ٱلرِّقَابِ وَ أَقَامَ ٱلصَّلَـٰوةَ وَءَاتَى ٱلزَّكَوٰةَ وَ

ٱلْمُوفُونَ بِعَهْدِهِمْ إِذَا عَـٰهَدُواْ وَ ٱلصَّـٰبِرِينَ فِى ٱلْبَأْسَآءِ وَ

ٱلضَّرَّآءِ وَحِينَ ٱلْبَأْسِ أُوْلَـٰئِكَ ٱلَّذِينَ صَدَقُواْ وَأُوْلَـٰئِكَ

هُمُ ٱلْمُتَّقُونَ

> It is not righteousness that you turn your faces
> toward the East or West; but it is righteousness to
> believe in Allah and the Last Day and the angels
> and the Book and the messengers; to spend of your
> substance out of love for Him for your kin, for
> orphans, for the needy, for the wayfarer, for those
> who ask, and for the ransom of slaves; to be
> steadfast in prayer and practice regular charity; to
> fulfil the contracts which you have made; and to be
> firm and patient in pain (or suffering) and adversity
> and throughout all periods of panic. Such are the
> people of truth, the God-fearing. (Al Baqarah,
> 2:177)

These general attributes will now be explicitly linked to the attributes
that Islamic leaders and followers should embrace.

Application of *birr* to leadership. Based on the above verses, several
moral attributes of righteous leaders become salient:

- They act justly and do not allow their personal feelings to hinder
  justice.
- They have *iman* since they believe in Allah, the Last Day, the
  angels, the Books and the messengers,
- They take care of those in need, and do so for the love of Allah,
- They are steadfast in prayer and practice charity,
- They observe all contracts, and

- They are patient no matter what type of adversity or personal suffering they may be experiencing.

In general, then, participants of all faiths in an organization are entitled to basic human decency and dignity and to be treated fairly. In an Islamic organization, a leader should be sensitive to others' needs — whether spiritual, material, physical, or psychological. The following hadith also stresses the importance of righteousness, and the multiplier effect that it has on a person's behavior. 'Abdullah reported that:

The Prophet (saw) said, "Truthfulness leads to righteousness, and righteousness leads to Paradise. A man continues to tell the truth until he becomes a truthful person. Falsehood leads to *fajur* (i.e., wickedness, evil-doing), and *fajur* (wickedness) leads to the Fire, and a man may continue to tell lies till he is written before Allah, a liar."[53]

4. *Mujāhada* or struggle within oneself toward self-improvement. This concept is portrayed very accurately by the following verses from the Qur'an:

يَـٰٓأَيُّهَا الَّذِينَ ءَامَنُوا ٱرْكَعُوا وَ ٱسْجُدُوا وَٱعْبُدُوا رَبَّكُمْ وَٱفْعَلُوا الْخَيْرَ لَعَلَّكُمْ تُفْلِحُونَ ۩

وَجَـٰهِدُوا فِى اللَّهِ حَقَّ جِهَادِهِ هُوَ ٱجْتَبَىٰكُمْ وَمَا جَعَلَ عَلَيْكُمْ فِى الدِّينِ مِنْ حَرَجٍ مِّلَّةَ أَبِيكُمْ إِبْرَٰهِيمَ هُوَ سَمَّىٰكُمُ الْمُسْلِمِينَ مِن قَبْلُ وَ فِى هَـٰذَا لِيَكُونَ الرَّسُولُ شَهِيدًا عَلَيْكُمْ وَتَكُونُوا شُهَدَآءَ عَلَى النَّاسِ فَأَقِيمُوا الصَّلَوٰةَ وَءَاتُوا الزَّكَوٰةَ وَ ٱعْتَصِمُوا بِاللَّهِ هُوَ مَوْلَىٰكُمْ فَنِعْمَ الْمَوْلَىٰ وَ نِعْمَ النَّصِيرُ ۞

O you who believe! Bow down, prostrate yourselves and adore your Lord, and do good that you may prosper. And strive in His cause as you ought to strive (with sincerity and under discipline): He has chosen you and has imposed no difficulties on you

---

[53] *Sahih al Bukhari*, 8.116.

in religion; it is the faith of your father Abraham. It
is He who has named you Muslims both before and
in this (revelation); that the Messenger may be a
witness for you and you be witnesses for mankind!
So establish regular prayer, give regular charity and
hold fast to Allah! He is your protector, the best to
protect and the best to help! (Al Hajj, 22:77–78)

The following two hadiths reinforce the importance of this inner
striving to improve oneself:

The Prophet (peace be upon him) said: A wise person is one who keeps
watch over his bodily desires and passions, checks himself from what is
harmful, and strives for what will benefit him after death; and a foolish
person is one who subordinates himself to his cravings and desires and
expects from Allah the fulfillment of his futile desires.[54]

And:

Allah's Messenger (saw) said, "The believers in the world are of three types:
those who believe in Allah and His Messenger and do not doubt, but strive
with their property and their persons in Allah's cause; those who people trust
with their property and their persons; and those who, when they are about to
display greed, abandon it for the sake of Allah, the Great and Glorious."[55]

The dimension of *mujāhadah* or inner struggle permeates the
progression from *iman* to *ihsān*, and continues thereafter.

Application of *mujāhadah* to leadership.   The principle of
mujahadah encapsulates the process of inner struggle or jihad toward
self-improvement.   Leaders and followers practicing *mujāhadah* are
continuously monitoring and evaluating their *niyāt* (intentions) and
actions. They work hard at practicing what they say, and encourage
others in this struggle:

$$\text{أَتَأْمُرُونَ ٱلنَّاسَ بِٱلْبِرِّ وَ تَنسَوْنَ أَنفُسَكُمْ وَ أَنتُمْ تَتْلُونَ}$$
$$\text{ٱلْكِتَٰبَ أَفَلَا تَعْقِلُونَ}$$

Do you enjoin right conduct on the people and
forget (to practice it) yourselves and yet you study
the Scripture?   Will you not understand? (Al
Baqarah, 2:44)

---

[54] Abu Ya'la ibn Shaddad ibn Aws, *Mishkat al Masabih,* 0066 (R), transmitted by
Tirmidhi.

[55] Abu Sa'id al Khudri, *Mishkat al Masabih,* 3854, transmitted by Ahmad.

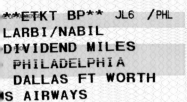

promise. All Muslims — whether leaders or d to keep their promises.

$$\text{يَـٰٓأَيُّهَا ٱلَّذِينَ ءَامَنُوٓاْ أَوْفُواْ بِٱلْعُقُودِ}$$

/ho believe! fulfil (all) obligations. (Al 5:1)

characterizes a Muslim. Breaking one's word 'ite is:

upon him) said, "The signs of a hypocrite are three: e tells a lie; whenever he promises, he breaks it (his m, he proves to be dishonest (if you entrust him with eturn it)."[56]

to **leadership**. Based upon the above discussion, ₃ very important for all, and a leader is not exempted from this important behavioral principle.

I bought something from the Prophet (*saw*) before he received his Prophetic commission, and as there was something still due to him I promised him that I would bring it to him at his place, but I forgot. When I remembered three days later, I went to that place and found him there. He said: You have vexed me, young man. I have been here for three days waiting for you.[57]

Islam, however, is quite understanding. In spite of the best of intentions, extenuating circumstances may prevent a Muslim leader or follower from keeping a promise.

The Prophet (*saw*) said: "When a man makes a promise to his brother with the *intention* of fulfilling it and does not do so, and does not come at the appointed time, he is guilty of no sin.[58]

Now that we have discussed the bases of Islamic leadership, we need to explore how to build upon them, and how to improve the effectiveness of Muslim leaders. To do so, we will now examine how to achieve a better fit between the leader, his or her followers, and the leadership situation.

---

[56] Abu Hurayrah, *Sahih al Bukhari*, hadith 1.32.

[57] 'Abdullah Ibn Abul Hamsa, in Abu Dawud.

[58] Zayd ibn Arqam, in Abu Dawud. Emphasis on *intention* was added by the authors.

In Focus 1: Cassam Uteem: The People's President

A few thousand kilometers off the east coast of Madagascar, in the middle of the Indian ocean, lies the island of Mauritius, a beautiful tropical paradise — the country that has as its President, Cassam Uteem.

Surrounded by deep blue lagoons, soft white beaches, and gorgeous coral reefs, Mauritius is about 720 square miles in size, and has a mixed population, numbering about 1.1 million inhabitants with Indians, Muslims, Chinese, Creoles and people of European descent living at peace with one another. Muslims are a minority, comprising about 17% of the population. Mauritius was a British colony until March 12, 1968 when it became independent. In 1992, Mauritius became a republic.

Like Mauritius's current Prime Minister, Dr. Navin Ramgoolam, President Uteem's ancestors came to this island about 133 years ago when the British took over India, and entire families were relocated to other British colonies as indentured labor to work in sugar cane plantations. It was very hard work, but little did they know what their descendants would accomplish in the future. Initially, a very active social worker, the country's accession to independence in 1968 marked Cassam Uteem's own transition to political involvement. He first served as Minister of Social Security, then as Lord Mayor of the capital city of Mauritius, Port Louis, before becoming the Minister of Industry and Industry Technology. In 1992, Cassam Uteem became the first Muslim President of Mauritius, and was recently reappointed to a second term in office.

In his capacity as a political leader in Parliament, he has worked very hard to restore trust and confidence among all segments of the population in Mauritius, especially after the disturbances that preceded this country's independence in 1968. First, instead of focusing on one segment of the population, he emphasized the all-encompassing philosophy of "Unity in Diversity." Again and again, he has stressed the theme of national unity, stating the following in one of his passionate pleas on this subject: "Equal opportunity for all, equal access to education, professional training, and meritocracy are the bases of a civil society, an egalitatarian society, and especially a united society." Second, he has led the fight against illegal drugs and substance abuse — an unwelcome consequence of Mauritius's improving economic conditions. Third, he has worked hard to emphasize education and positive change. Mauritius now has a literacy rate of 82.9 percent. Finally, he has fought long and hard for workers' rights.

President Uteem is a *musulman convaincu* (a staunch Muslim), and has always been quite involved in activities involving Muslims. For example, he used to broadcast radio programs on Islam. He was instrumental in helping establish the IWF, the Islamic Welfare Foundation — an organization dedicated to helping the poor and needy, and to promoting education through the pooling of *zakat* donations. He belonged to both the Muslim Youth Federation and contributed significantly to the efforts of the Students' Islamic Movement. In fact, his activities with respect to Islam have been well received by Mauritians of all faiths.

As president, Br. Uteem has been the very symbol of humility and dignity. One incident that has particularly inspired him relates to 'Umar (*ra*). When 'Umar (*ra*) went to sign the treaty signaling the capture of Jerusalem, he could hardly be recognized from his small group of attendants. In fact, when he went to Jerusalem with his servant, they had one camel on which each of them rode by turn. When 'Umar (*ra*) was entering Jerusalem it happened to be the servant's turn to ride on the camel. Though the servant offered his turn to the *khalifah*, 'Umar refused and remarked: "The honor of Islam (i.e., being a Muslim) is enough for all of us." He entered Jerusalem holding the rope of the camel on which [his servant] was riding.

This example of humility and modesty inspired President Uteem's life. Unlike many other heads of state, he does not live in the Presidential Palace. He only uses it for his office, keeping the doors open to everyone, including the poorest sugarcane laborers. When someone wanted to write a book about him, he tried to dissuade the person, and the biographer had to cull facts from Uteem's writings and speeches. Every letter written to him always receives an answer. His integrity is beyond compare. In the words of his wife, he is *un homme droit*, "a man of principle." Once he helped a student from a poor family. The mother of the student was so pleased that she came to visit him at home. He was away, and she left him a pen as a gift. When he came home, Cassam Uteem was unhappy when he found the pen. He did not want to take it. Why? He is a man who will never accept any reward for helping people.

President Uteem believes that the Republic of Mauritius can only grow and prosper by accepting the fact of cultural diversity, and that Mauritians in general and Muslims in particular can only progress by learning about their differences as well as by reinforcing the values that they share in common. He believes in collegial leadership — he wants to see a united Mauritius, not the splintering of Mauritian society.

Indeed the task of nation-building is not yet completed, and his presidency has been, and still is, animated by the quest to provide what is best for the people of his country: the spread of liberty, the expansion of economic prosperity without the destruction of the environment, justice in the distribution of wealth, and accountability and ethics in both the public and private sectors. For him, multiculturality can only thrive in an open society where the political environment enables full participation and open interaction of all the diverse elements. He is the president of the people, but at heart he is still the social worker who has assumed the role of president. Finally, his bid to transcend cultural specificity to inhabit the realm of universal ideas reminds us that in so doing, he is behaving exactly as he should as a Muslim. After all, is he not living a critical Qur'anic injunction, expressed as *li ta'ārafū* (to get to know one another)? — an injunction that Allah has addressed to mankind as a whole, not just to Muslims only. Indeed, Allah says in *Surah Hujurat* (49:13):

> O mankind, we have created you from a single pair
> of a male and female, and have made you into
> nations and tribes that you may know one another.

Chapter 3
The Locus of Leadership

The nature of leadership can best be understood by examining the transactions between a leader and his or her followers within the context of a specific situation.[59] As shown in Figure 3-1, leadership is a process involving three factors: the leader, the follower, and the situation. The better the match among the characteristics of the leader, the followers, and the situation, the more effective will be the leader. The *locus of leadership* is the area where these three factors intersect. A leader is most effective when he is functioning within the locus of leadership. To understand how a leader can improve his leadership skills requires that we examine these three factors in detail.

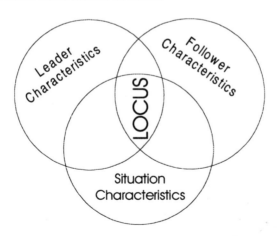

Figure 3-1: Locus of Leadership

---

[59] Hollander, E. P. (1978). *Leadership Dynamics*. New York, NY: Free Press.

Leader Characteristics

The characteristics of an Islamic leader affect his or her behavior. They include his or her personality, moral character (as discussed in Chapter 2), motives, degree of competency, and goals. In their book, *The Leadership Challenge*, Kouzes and Posner, two leadership researchers, surveyed 2,615 of the most successful leaders in the United States in order to identify what characteristics made them so effective. Table 3-1 presents a list of the top eight characteristics that followers look for in a leader.

Table 3-1: Characteristics of Effective Leaders[60]

Characteristic	Ranking	Percent of respondents
Honest	1	83
Competent	2	67
Forward-looking	3	62
Inspiring	4	58
Intelligent	5	43
Fair-minded	6	40
Straightforward	7	37
Imaginative	8	34

The characteristics of effective leaders from Kouzes and Posner's study are remarkably Islamic. Let us discuss the top four characteristics here.

- *Honesty:* Leaders are considered honest to the extent that there is "consistency between word and deed." In other words, they have integrity and do what they say they are going to do. In the Qur'an, the Prophet Musa[61] (*as*) is described as "strong and trustworthy" (*al-*

---

[60] Kouzes, J. and Posner, B. (1995). *The Leadership Challenge: How to Get Extraordinary Things Done in Organizations*. San Francisco, CA: Jossey-Bass, p. 17.

[61] Musa (*as*) is the arabic equivalent of Moses (*as*).

qawi al-amīn) by one of the young ladies[62] and the Prophet Yusuf (*as*) is described as one who is truthful.[63] Similarly, the Prophet Muhammad's (*saw*) two names are especially relevant. When he was still a youth, the Quraish used to call him *Sādiq* (Truthful) and *Amīn* (Trustworthy), and he was respected by all, even the chiefs of Makkah. These qualities are emphasized by the following hadith narrated by 'Adi bin 'Amira al Kindi:

> I heard the Messenger of Allah (*saw*) say: "Whoso from you is appointed by us to a position of authority and he conceals from us a needle or something smaller than that, it would be misappropriation (of public funds), and he will (have to) produce (it) on the Day of Judgment."[64]

Muslim leaders should be honest not only because it makes them better leaders, but also because they are accountable for their deeds to Allah both in this world and in the hereafter.

Why is honesty and integrity so important with respect to leaders? Although Kouzes and Posner (1987) do not provide the reader with an answer, Islam does. Leadership is more than an assignment or a job; it is a *trust* — whatever the circumstance may be. Both in matters of *dīn* as well as life in general, this emphasis can be easily observed. For example, one Muslim-owned company includes *amānah* at the core of its set of corporate values, and stresses that the duties assigned to a manager (or any other employee) represent a trust, and should be fulfilled accordingly. Again, 'Umar (*ra*) as well Abu Bakr (*ra*) saw their fundamental responsibility as honoring the trust placed in them by the Ummah, and they were extremely sincere and diligent in fulfilling this trust.

* *Competence:* People are more likely to follow a leader's directives if they believe that this person knows what he or she is doing. If followers doubt the capabilities of their leader, they will be less enthusiastic in accepting directions from him. Competency does not relate only to the current technical skills of the leader; his past record of accomplishment as a leader affects others' perception of his competence. As discussed in Chapter 2, a competent but Islamically weak leader may be preferred to an incompetent leader that is more knowledgeable Islamically. Of course, a leader who is both competent and Islamically strong is to be given priority.

---

[62] See Qassas, 28:26.
[63] See Yusuf, 12:46.
[64] *Sahih Muslim,* hadith 4514.

In general, Islamic leaders must be careful not to lead from a position of weakness. How many times have we witnessed the appointment of an excellent *imam* to the position of president in a Muslim organization only to watch him struggle later? As suggested by Figure 3-1, a leader who is competent in one situation may not be competent in another. The Prophet (*saw*), except in matters where he had received *wahy*, would often seek and follow the advice of his companions. As Afzalur Rahman indicates, "This enabled all his men to take part in discussion and offer suggestions, and in this way the best solution was found by mutual consultation."[65] For example, at the battle of Badr, Muhammad (*saw*) consulted all parties, among both the *Ansār* and the *Muhājirun*, with respect to the advancing forces of the Quraish, and selected the place of fighting on the advice of Al Hubab bin al Mundhir. The strategy of draining the well closest to the enemy and filling it up with sand was also suggested by the same companion and agreed to by the Prophet Muhammad (*saw*).[66] In matters of *dīn*, the Prophet's (*saw*) competence cannot be doubted; in other matters of *dunya* where he had not received divine guidance, he sought and accepted advice from others. The following hadith indicates the Prophet's (*saw*) awareness of his strengths and limitations:

I and Allah's Messenger (peace be upon him) happened to pass by people near the date-palm trees. He (the Prophet) said: What are these people doing? They said: They are cross polinating, i.e., they combine the male with the female (tree) and thus they yield more fruit. Thereupon Allah's Messenger (peace be upon him) said: I do not find it to be of any use. The people were informed about it and they abandoned this practice. Allah's Messenger (peace be upon him) was later on informed that the yield had dwindled, whereupon he said: If there is any use of it, then they should do it, for it was just a personal opinion of mine, and do not go after my personal opinion, but when I say to you anything on behalf of Allah, then do accept it, for I do not attribute lieing to Allah, the Exalted and Glorious.[67]

Most importantly, Islam draws a distinction between knowledge (*'ilm*) and one's ability to put this knowledge into practice (*hikmah*). Whereas competence relates more to *ilm*, the Islamic perspective of

---

[65] Rahman, p. 170.
[66] Haykal, pp. 223–224.
[67] Narrated by Talhah ibn Ubaydullah, *Sahih Muslim*, Hadith 5830.

leadership recognizes the importance of both, and emphasizes that both should be present for a leader to be effective.[68]

$$و\ \ لَمَّا\ بَلَغَ\ أَشُدَّهُ\ وَٱسْتَوَىٰٓ\ ءَاتَيْنَٰهُ\ حُكْمًا\ وَعِلْمًا\ وَكَذَٰلِكَ$$

$$نَجْزِى\ ٱلْمُحْسِنِينَ$$

> When he (Musa) reached full age and was firmly established (in life) We bestowed on him wisdom and knowledge: for thus do We reward those who do good. (Qassas, 28:14)

Muslim leaders must endeavor to acquire practical knowledge as well as the capability for applying it in appropriate situations.

- *Having a vision and being forward-looking:* Leaders are expected to have a sense of direction and a long-term vision for their organization or community. One of the reasons why the Muslim Students' Association of the USA and Canada was so successful initially was because the leaders of the organization had a clear vision of what the organization intended to accomplish. This vision was clearly outlined in MSA pamphlets, and enthusiastically shared by its membership. MSA has recently updated its vision statement, which reads as follows: *"To be the medium through which Islam will be the active and progressive force on University and College campuses throughout North America."* Safi[69] suggests that a well-articulated vision brings constancy to the leader's directives and stability to the organization, inspires organizational members, and reduces the potential for confusion and conflict among all stakeholders. Most importantly, a vision acts as a cognitive frame of reference for orchestrating all of the organization's activities.

Note that the vision itself does not have to be a completely original idea. It can be very simple, but it should be something that all can identify with. As one Muslim leader once taught one of this book's co-authors, the vision should constantly inspire all of a leader's and his followers' efforts. Whether at work or at rest, whether in failure or success, this vision should be what propels all organizational members forward. Even if they are not immediately able to enact it,

---

[68] Safi, Louay (1995). "Leadership and Subordination: An Islamic Perspective." *American Journal of Islamic Social Sciences*, Summer, vol. 12, 2, pp. 204–223.
[69] Ibid.

they should always be moving toward the future state described by
the vision, and trust in Allah to make it happen.

* *Inspiration:* Followers expect their leaders to remain positive about
the future no matter how bad the situation may be. The leader must
never give up or lose hope. During the battles of Badr, Uhud and
Hunain, Muhammad (*saw*) neither flinched in front of larger hostile
forces, nor panicked even when Muslim forces were retreating in
disarray. Another example of how a leader inspires his followers
comes from Abu Bakr (*ra*). After the death of the Prophet (*saw*),
Muslims were in shock. 'Umar (*ra*) was especially distraught; he
believed firmly that Muhammad (*saw*) did not die, and was
proclaiming this fact loudly. Abu Bakr (*ra*) calmed him down,
saying, "Softly, O 'Umar! Keep silent!" and then delivered the
following address:

O People, if you have been worshipping Muhammad, then know that
Muhammad is dead. But if you have been worshipping Allah, then know that
Allah is living and never dies.[70]

He then recited the following verse from the Qur'an:

$$\text{وَمَا مُحَمَّدٌ إِلاَّ رَسُولٌ قَدْ خَلَتْ مِن قَبْلِهِ ٱلرُّسُلُ}$$

$$\text{أَفَإِيْن مَّاتَ أَوْ قُتِلَ ٱنقَلَبْتُمْ عَلَىٰٓ أَعْقَـٰبِكُمْ وَمَن}$$

$$\text{يَنقَلِبْ عَلَىٰ عَقِبَيْهِ فَلَن يَضُرَّ ٱللَّهَ شَيْئًا وَسَيَجْزِي}$$

$$\text{ٱللَّهُ ٱلشَّـٰكِرِينَ}$$

> Muhammad is no more than a Messenger: many
> were the messengers that passed away before him.
> If he died or were slain, will you then turn back on
> your heels? If any did turn back on his heels, not
> the least harm will he do to Allah; but Allah (on the
> other hand) will swiftly reward those who (serve
> him) with gratitude. (Al 'Imran, 3:144)

This inspiring address soothed the people's grief, and enabled them
to remain positive and focused.

In addition to the above characteristics of effective leaders derived
from current empirical research on leadership, Islam encourages

---

[70] Haykal, pp. 506–7.

Muslims to emulate some additional attributes if one is to become an effective leader. Assuming that the leader is already strong in his moral character, here are further important Islamic characteristics that a leader needs to develop in himself.

- *Strength of character:* A leader needs to abstain from actions prohibited by Islam and keep away from evil company. Because of the need for him to be an excellent role model for other Muslims and to persevere and inspire both in good and bad situations, he cannot allow himself to succumb to wordly temptations. In other words, strength of character is a must for a leader, especially during hard times. After the Prophet's death, it was Abu Bakr's (*ra*) strength of character that enabled him to weather dissent from apostates.[71]

- *Patience (*sabr*):* It is one of the defining characteristics of Islamic leadership. In a verse of the Qur'an, Allah explicitly identifies patience as one of the two key attributes of leadership:

$$\text{وَجَعَلْنَا مِنْهُمْ أَئِمَّةً يَهْدُونَ بِأَمْرِنَا لَمَّا صَبَرُواْ وَكَانُواْ بِآيَٰتِنَا يُوقِنُون}$$

> And We appointed from among them leaders giving guidance under Our command so long as they persevered with patience and continued to have faith in Our signs. (Sajdah, 32:24)

Indeed, like all other believers, a leader can expect to be tested, and he will need to endure these trials calmly and without losing faith.

$$\text{وَ لَنَبْلُوَنَّكُم بِشَىْءٍ مِّنَ ٱلْخَوْفِ وَ ٱلْجُوعِ وَنَقْصٍ مِّنَ ٱلْأَمْوَٰلِ وَ ٱلْأَنفُسِ وَٱلثَّمَرَٰتِ وَبَشِّرِ ٱلصَّٰبِرِين}$$

> Be sure We shall test you with something of fear and hunger some loss in goods or lives or the fruits (of your toil) but give glad tidings to those who patiently persevere. (Al Baqarah, 2:155)

The example of the Prophet (*saw*) and early converts to Islam during the boycott of the Muslims in Makkah illustrates the need for *sabr*.

---

[71] Safi, p. 216.

As Safi points out, *sabr* is the type of endurance leaders need during natural disasters ordained by Allah. Should the source of suffering be human, then Allah enjoins resolve (*'azm*) and forbearance (*hilm*) upon Muslims.[72] Such forms of patience are what the prophets (*as*) demonstrate in their struggle against oppression and corruption.

- *Humility:* A leader needs to be humble, and must never let his ego get the better of him. In fact, the Qur'an describes Muslims in general as "those who walk on the earth with humility" (25:63).

Similarly, 'Ali (*ra*), in his letter to Malik al Ashtar al Nakha'i, strongly encourages him to remain humble in his new position as Governor of Egypt, and explains to him why pride and arrogance are to be avoided.

Never say to yourself, "I am their Lord, their ruler ... and I must be obeyed submissively and humbly." Such a thought will unbalance your mind, will make you vain and arrogant, will weaken your faith in religion and will make you seek the support of any power other than Allah's (perhaps that of your party or your government). If your rule makes you feel pride or vanity over your subjects, then think of the Lord's ... creations, the supremacy of His might and glory, His power to do things that you cannot even dream of doing, and His control over you which is more dominating than you can ever achieve yourself over anything around you.[73]

While preparing for the battle of Al Ahzab, the Prophet Muhammad (*saw*) joined the Companions in digging the ditch around Madinah and carried bowls of earth on his head. He did not stay aloof. Hence, good leaders are also able to follow the very directives they give to their followers.

- *Kindness and magnanimity:* A leader's role is not one of a policeman wielding a big stick. The Prophet Muhammad (*saw*) said:

Avert the infliction of prescribed penalties on Muslims as much as you can, and if there is any way, let a man go, for it is better for a leader to make a mistake in forgiving than to make a mistake in punishing.[74]

'Umar (*ra*) was quoted as saying to the people:

I have appointed over you governors and agents not to beat your bodies or take your monies, but rather to teach you and serve you.[75]

---

[72] Safi, p. 218 citing Ahqāf, 46:35.
[73] Behzadnia and Denny, p. 8.
[74] Aisha, transmitted by Tirmidhi, hadith 3570.
[75] Al Buraey, Muhammad (1985). *Administrative Development: An Islamic Perspective.* London, UK: KPI, p. 248.

Realizing that distribution of the conquered lands in Iraq, Syria, and Egypt to the Muslim army could destabilize the agricultural infrastructure of these countries, 'Umar did not follow the historical precedents of the time. Rather, he allowed the inhabitants of these areas to keep their lands, but collected taxes: *zakat* from Muslim and *jizyah* from non-Muslim citizens. This balanced policy and gentle approach guaranteed a regular source of revenue to the Islamic State.[76]

- *Self-understanding:* Self-understanding is the ability to recognize one's strengths and compensate for one's weaknesses. Islamic organizations that have done a good job at developing workers and leaders have placed an emphasis on putting together challenging situations for promising recruits. These recruits receive feedback from their peers, and the feedback becomes the basis for helping them increase their self-understanding. Abu Bakr (*ra*) understood the importance of self-understanding and feedback. Upon the occasion of his first khutbah as Caliph, he stated:

  0 people! I have been selected as your trustee although I am no better than anyone of you. If I am right, obey me. If I am misguided, set me right.[77]

- *The willingness to seek consultation:* Depending on their leadership style, leaders may find it easy or difficult to consult others. Islam, however, stresses consultation in all affairs. Through the Qur'anic phrase *amruhum shura baynahum* (who conduct their affairs through mutual consultation) (42:38) and the Prophet's (*saw*) habit of seeking and accepting advice, the limits on the exercise of power have been set forth by the Qur'an and the sunnah. As Al Buraey points out, *shura* plays a critical role in administration and management, specifically with respect to decision-making; it provides a restraint on administrative power and authority.[78] Unlike the elitist (majority/minority) approaches to decision-making, the concept of *shura* stresses consensus building. This process of consensus building as applied by Muslim leaders need *not* be confined to elite or special interest groups alone; instead, it should be extended to include all affected by the expected decisions, especially when the subject of consultation does not require specialized "technical" knowledge or experience.

---

[76] Al Buraey, pp. 250–1.
[77] *Islamic Scholar*, Prominent Muslims.
[78] Al Buraey, Muhammad, p. 320.

- *Equity and impartiality:* A key attribute of an Islamic leader is equity and impartiality. In dealing with others, the leader must be impartial to all, whether they are Muslim or not. The following event about Fayruz al Daylami, a well-known companion of the Prophet (*saw*) illustrates the importance of this attribute.

  [After being summoned by 'Umar (*ra*)], Fayruz al Daylami went to Madinah and sought an audience with 'Umar. 'Umar granted him permission. Evidently there was a crowd waiting to see 'Umar and a Quraysh youth pushed Fayruz. Fayruz raised his hand and hit the Quraysh youth on the nose. The youth went to 'Umar who asked: "Who did this to you?"

  "Fayruz. He is at the door," said the youth. Fayruz entered and 'Umar asked: "What is this, O Fayruz?"

  "O Amir al-Muminin," said Fayruz. "You wrote to me. You didn't write to him. You gave me permission to enter and you didn't give him permission. He wanted to enter in my turn before me. Then I did what you have been told."

  "*Al Qisas,*" pronounced 'Umar in judgment, meaning that Fayruz had to receive the same blow from the youth in retaliation. "Must it be so?" asked Fayruz. "It must be so," insisted 'Umar.

  Fayruz then got down on his knees and the youth stood up to exact his retaliation.[79]

- *Modesty and simplicity:* In contrast to Western theories of leadership and management that stay silent on the topic, Islam stresses modesty. When 'Umar (*ra*) went to sign the treaty signaling the capture of Jerusalem, he could hardly be recognized from his small group of attendants. Here is a description of 'Umar (*ra*) as he approached Jerusalem:

  His clothes were dirty and there were several patches on them. Abu 'Ubaidah, Khalid bin Walid, and other commanders came some distance to receive him. They were wearing costly garments. This made 'Umar (*ra*) angry. He threw some pebbles at his generals (to show his anger) and said, "Have you changed so much in just two years? The only way [to] success is the way of the Holy Prophet (*saw*)."[80]

---

[79] *Winalim* (1996). Silver Springs, MD: ISL Software Corporation, "Biographies of Companions."

[80] *Islamic Scholar* software, Prominent Muslims. For additional details on this incident in 'Umar's (*ra*) life, please see page 35 earlier in the vignette about President Cassam Uteem.

He lived in a simple house. He had no bodyguards for his personal security, and walked the streets of Madinah without an escort.[81]

- *Good leaders are good followers:* Leaders must be willing to abide by the same rules that apply to their followers. At the battle of the Trench, the Prophet (*saw*) worked with those who were digging the ditch. Khalid ibn Walid, one of the best military leaders in the history of Islam, was always willing to do what ordinary soldiers do. During the expedition of Mu'tah, he fought as a regular soldier under the command of Zaid ibn Thabit. At a later occasion, at 'Umar's (*ra*) request, he gracefully agreed to step down as leader of the army but continued to fight as hard in the role of a regular soldier as he had when he had commanded the Muslim army.[82]

- *Responsibility:* According to the Islamic perspective of leadership, the leader is responsible for his followers' well-being. By accepting his position as leader, he has also accepted certain duties. One of the most important duties of a leader is that he is responsible for securing the legitimate rights of his community. As discussed with respect to the servant-leader and guardian-leader roles, the concept of responsibility is tied to various aspects of leadership in Islam, and a leader who fails to take care of one's members or followers will have to answer for it to Allah Himself.

Leadership Styles

Besides the characteristics of leaders, we also need to focus on the styles that effective leaders use in dealing with followers. Researchers have identified two basic styles: *directive* or task-oriented and *participative* or employee-oriented. Leaders who use a directive style of leadership instruct and closely supervise their followers to make sure that the tasks are performed to their expectations. This type of leader is more concerned with getting the job done rather than with mentoring and coaching his or her followers. Conversely, leaders with a participative style of leadership try to involve instead of direct their followers; by so doing, they contribute to their personal growth, and increase their level of motivation. Over time, they endeavor to establish friendly and trusting relationships with their followers, taking a personal interest in their growth and development. Participative leaders tend to put less

---

[81] Faqih, I. (1988). *Glimpses of Islamic History*. Delhi, India: Adam Publishers and Distributors, p. 96, 107.
[82] Safi, 221.

emphasis on the use of legitimate and coercive power. Leaders who are high in both directive and participative styles of leadership have a team-oriented style whereas leaders who are low in both have a laissez-faire or free-rein style.   Between these two basic styles is any number of combinations, i.e., varying degrees of being directive and/or participative.

Initially, the Ohio State studies research[83] showed that leaders who are rated high in a directive style of leadership tend to be associated with higher rates of grievances and higher turnover from their employees as compared to leaders rated high in a participative or employee-oriented style. More recent research indicates that effective leaders exhibit both types of styles, and that their effectiveness is a function of the situation as well as the characteristics of their followers.[84]

Assess your leadership style: please turn to page 56 at the end of this chapter, and assess your own leadership style. Then go to page 57, and evaluate yourself.

Question: Do you agree with the results of the leadership style question-naire? Why or why not?

Follower Characteristics

As indicated in Figure 3-1, follower characteristics represent an important ingredient in the leadership process. Just as in the case of their leader, the characteristics of Muslim followers affect their behavior and include personality attributes, moral character, motives, degree of competency, and goals. Many of their characteristics correspond to the ones described above except for obedience, dynamic "followership" and unity, which are described below.

- *Obedience:* Whether during conditions of peace or war, the leader must be obeyed. Ibn 'Umar reported Allah's messenger (*saw*) as saying, "Hearing and obeying are the duty of a Muslim, both

---

[83] Stogdill, R. M. and Coons, A. E., eds (1957). *Leader Behavior: Its Description and Measurement.* Columbus, OH: The Ohio State University Bureau of Business Research.

[84] Hellriegel, Don and Slocum, John (1992). *Management.* Reading, Mass: Addison-Wesley, p. 478.

regarding what he likes and what he dislikes."[85] The Qur'an clearly states:

$$\text{يَـٰٓأَيُّهَا ٱلَّذِينَ ءَامَنُوٓاْ أَطِيعُواْ ٱللَّهَ وَ أَطِيعُواْ ٱلرَّسُولَ}$$

$$\text{وَأُوْلِى ٱلْأَمْرِ مِنكُمْ فَإِن تَنَـٰزَعْتُمْ فِى شَىْءٍ فَرُدُّوهُ}$$

$$\text{إِلَى ٱللَّهِ وَٱلرَّسُولِ إِن كُنتُمْ تُؤْمِنُونَ بِٱللَّهِ وَٱلْيَوْمِ ٱلْأَخِرِ}$$

$$\text{ذَٰلِكَ خَيْرٌ وَ أَحْسَنُ تَأْوِيلاً}$$

> O you who believe! Obey Allah, and obey the
> Messenger, and those charged with authority among
> you. If you differ in anything among yourselves
> refer it to Allah and His Messenger if you do
> believe in Allah and the Last Day: that is best and
> most suitable for final determination. (Al Nisā',
> 4:59)

The consequences of a lack of obedience to the leader can easily be seen in the Muslim debacle at Uhud after the archers abandoned their posts in spite of explicit and unequivocal instructions from the Prophet (*saw*).

Obedience is also required of the whole organization or community. As Muhammad Asad indicates, after a leader has been duly elected, he may "be considered to have received a pledge of allegiance (*bay'ah*) from the community." As a result, both the majority who voted for him as well as the minority who may have voted against him now owe him obedience and allegiance. The Prophet (*saw*) said:

> The hand of Allah is upon the community [*al jama'ah*]; and he who sets
> himself apart from it will be set apart in the hellfire. He who departs from the
> community [*faraqa al jama'ah*] by [even] a handspan ceases to be a Muslim
> [literally "throws off Islam from his neck"][86]

In fact, Islam considers obedience to the leader so important that it views any kind of insubordination to be abhorrent except in very specific circumstances. Again, the Prophet (*saw*) said:

---

[85] Rahman, A., p. 75.

[86] Asad, M. (1985). *The Principles of State and Government in Islam*. Gibraltrar: Dar Al-Andalus, p. 69.

The best of your rulers are those whom you love and who love you, who invoke Allah's blessings upon you and you invoke His blessings upon them. And the worst of your rulers are those whom you hate and who hate you and whom you curse and who curse you. It was asked (by those present): Shouldn't we overthrow them with the help of the sword? He said: No, as long as they establish prayer among you. If you then find anything detestable in them, you should hate their administration, but do not withdraw yourselves from their obedience.[87]

- *Dynamic followership:* Although Islam emphasizes that followers should comply with the directives of their leader, it does not condone blind subservience. Once a person stood up in a public meeting and said, "O 'Umar, fear Allah." The audience tried to stop him but 'Umar said, "Let him speak, he is free to give his opinion. If people do not give their opinions they are useless and if we (the rulers) do not listen to them, we are useless." This is why 'Umar was asked on one occasion to explain where he obtained a long dress when everyone else had received a short dress.[88] Both men and women enjoy this freedom of opinion. On another occasion, 'Umar (*ra*) was suggesting the quantity of dowry to be fixed at the time of *nikah* (marriage ceremony). What he said was not in accordance with Islamic principles. A lady immediately stood up and said, "O 'Umar, fear Allah." Hearing her sound argument based on the Qur'an, 'Umar (*ra*) realized his mistake and said, "The lady is right and the leader of the Muslims (himself) is wrong."[89] 'Umar's behavior illustrates clearly that followers in Islam are not to be passive bystanders should the leader err. His example is clearly supported by what the Prophet (peace be upon him) said:

The best fighting (jihad) in the path of Allah is (to speak) a word of justice to an oppressive ruler.[90]

Unity: The above discussion on obedience does not explain why Islam views it as so important. Obedience is important partly because Muslims need to stay united. Muslim followers must remain

---

[87] Reported by Awf ibn Malik in *Sahih Muslim.*

[88] Al Habshi, Syed Othman. (1987) "Development of Islamic Managerial and Administrative Practices: A Historical Perspective." In *Seminar on Islamic Management.* Edited by the Training Division of the Islamic Research and Training Institute. Malaysia, Kuala Lumpur, p. 17. It was later known that 'Umar's son, 'Abdullah, had given his father his share.

[89] Shibli-Nu'mani, Shamsul 'Ulama A. (1957). *Omar the Great: The Second Caliph of Islam.* Vols. 1 and 2, 2nd Revision. Translated by Maulana Zafar Ali Khan. Pakistan: Lahore, Sh. Muhammad Ashraf. Cited in Al-Buraey, p. 82.

[90] *Sunan of Abu-Dawood.* Hadith 4330, Narrated by Abu Sa'id al Khudri.

united in order to achieve their common objective(s). Current literature on organization strategy has emphasized repeatedly the need for organization participants to focus on a common set of organizational objectives if they are to succeed in the long term.[91] Internal fragmentation and a lack of unity may lead to the formation of divisive goals and organizational or community decline. Accordingly, the Qur'an has stressed the importance of unity among Muslims:

وَاعۡتَصِمُواْ بِحَبۡلِ ٱللَّهِ جَمِيعًا وَلَا تَفَرَّقُواْ وَاذۡكُرُواْ نِعۡمَتَ ٱللَّهِ عَلَيۡكُمۡ إِذۡ كُنتُمۡ أَعۡدَآءً فَأَلَّفَ بَيۡنَ قُلُوبِكُمۡ فَأَصۡبَحۡتُم بِنِعۡمَتِهِۦ إِخۡوَٰنًا وَكُنتُمۡ عَلَىٰ شَفَا حُفۡرَةٍ مِّنَ ٱلنَّارِ فَأَنقَذَكُم مِّنۡهَا كَذَٰلِكَ يُبَيِّنُ ٱللَّهُ لَكُمۡ ءَايَٰتِهِۦ لَعَلَّكُمۡ تَهۡتَدُونَ

> And hold fast, all together, by the rope which Allah (stretches out for you), and be not divided among yourselves; and remember with gratitude Allah's favor on you; for you were enemies and He joined your hearts in love so that by His grace you became brethren; and you were on the brink of the pit of fire and He saved you from it. Thus does Allah make his signs clear to you: that you may be guided. (Al Imran, 3:103)

Leaders are few; followers are many and diverse. To be more effective, leaders also need to understand and work with their followers. Identifying what types of followers are under a leader's charge is an important task for two reasons. First, a leader may have to adjust his leadership style depending upon the type of follower he or she is dealing with. Second, followers too, affect the leadership process; an important study of leader-follower relationships found that leaders may actually react to the performance of their followers rather than initiate it.[92]

---

[91] Thompson, A. and Strickland, A. (1993). *Strategic Management: Concepts and Cases.* Ill: Burr Ridge.

[92] Greene, C. N. (1975). "The Reciprocal Nature of Influence between Leader and Subordinate." *Journal of Applied Psychology*, 60: 187–193.

Hence, leadership is a reciprocal process. Leaders can influence the goals, perceptions, and behavior of their followers, but the reverse is also true.

Figure 3-2: Types of Followers

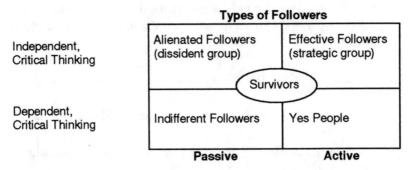

As shown in Figure 3-2, followers are not homogeneous: there are five types of followers in most Islamic organizations. The *alienated followers* represent members who are potentially disruptive. They are able to think independently and critically, but stay away because they are disenchanted as a result of previous incidents or because of personal enmity. The *indifferent followers* simply do not want to, or cannot, be involved. While these individuals may feel the need for social companionship, they shun any form of commitment. They follow the leader's directives, but they neither think critically nor are very active.

By contrast, the *yes people* followers are active, but do not think independently or critically. They support the leader enthusiastically, but do not question the leader's ideas or actions. Please note that Islam encourages followers to be *actively obedient* by providing them the opportunity to participate in *shura* and even to criticize the leader when he goes astray. Islamic followers are not expected to be subservient. The exchange described earlier between 'Umar (*ra*) and a woman on the subject of dowry illustrates this point vividly.[93] *Survivors* are the "Friday attendants" you find in Islamic associations. They are the least disruptive and generally play safe. They represent the greatest area of opportunity. Of course, they "believe," but they are not active. The leader needs to motivate them and to explain what needs to be done.

Effective followers are readily identifiable by six characteristics:

---

[93] Al Buraey, p. 82.

1. They practice Islam conscientiously, and therefore are honest, trustworthy, and brave.
2. They practice self-management and self-responsibility.
3. They can be delegated to, and will perform their tasks well with almost no supervision.
4. They are committed to the cause and to the organization.
5. They are critical in their thinking without being disrespectful or self-serving.
6. They do not waste their leader's and their organization's time and resources.

Effective followers are rarely born that way. It takes time to nurture a survivor or an indifferent follower into an effective follower. The Prophet (*saw*) was able to transform polytheist pagans into some of the best Muslims the world has ever seen, but he did so slowly and patiently. Developing effective followers is worthwhile because they facilitate the delegation process, which enables the leader to do more. *Effective followers* are also a good source of future leaders, thus providing continuity to the Islamic organization.

Assess your follower style: please go to page 58 at the end of this chapter, and assess your effectiveness as a follower. Then turn to page 59, and evaluate yourself.

Question: Do you agree with the results of the follower style questionnaire? Why or why not? Are there differences between your answers to the leadership and the followership questionnaires? Why or why not?

Situation Characteristics

The third factor that affects the leadership process relates to situation characteristics (see Figure 3-1). Before describing these, we must point out that how the situation will affect the leader depends on his or her perception of what is happening. Thus, a leader who believes that his or her followers are lazy and lack the necessary skills will interact with them on that basis. Accordingly, for the leader to shift to a more appropriate style of leadership, he or she will first have to modify his or her perception of the situation.

Researchers have identified several situational factors associated with leadership effectiveness:[94]

- *Leader-member relations* determine the degree to which the leader is accepted by the organization. When the organizational climate is good and members trust and respect the leader, then the situation is favorable to the leader. Conversely, when the leader is rejected by and does not get along with the members, he may have more difficulty working with them.

- *Task structure* describes how simple and routine a task is. Mailing fundraising letters is a routine task, and detailed instructions are sufficient to guide organizational members in performing it. Writing a constitution for an Islamic organization is a complex and nonroutine task. In this situation, the leader may not be able to come up with specific guidelines. Operating procedures will have to be more flexible, and the leader will have to assume a greater role in guiding the process.

- *Work group characteristics* may also affect how a leader's style is accepted. The leader needs to adjust his style according to the workgroup's stage of development. For example, if a workgroup is in its initial orientation phase,[95] he may be more directive and task-oriented than when the group has become more cohesive and autonomous.

- *The organization's climate and policies* may determine how "Islamically-oriented" the organization is. In an Islamic organization with the proper climate, the leader may not have to actively monitor members' behavior to check for consistency with Islamic values. By contrast, in organizations, which have more a "social" agenda, a leader may have an uphill fight. In a work environment with few rules and high task uncertainty, such as the development of a strategic plan for ISNA (the Islamic Society of North America), the leader may behave in a very participative manner with organization members.

- *The maturity level of members* relates to their ability to set challenging but achievable goals and their willingness to accept responsibility for achieving these goals.[96] Maturity relates

---

[94] Fiedler, F. E. (1967). *A Theory of Leadership Effectiveness.* New York, NY: McGraw-Hill.

[95] Gersick, C. (1988). "Time and Transition in Work Teams: Toward a New Model of Group Development." *Academy of Management Review,* March, pp. 9–41.

[96] Hersey, P. and Blanchard, K. H. (1988). *Management of Organizational Behavior.* 5th edition, Englewood Cliffs, NJ: Prentice-Hall.

specifically to the task being undertaken. Again, a leader may need to adjust his style of leadership to fit the maturity level of his followers. This aspect of leadership will be discussed in more detail later in this book, but here is an example from the *sīrah* of the Prophet (*saw*) of how he tailored a task to fit the specific characteristics of one of his companions, Hudhayfah ibn al Yaman, during the danger-prone period of early Islam.

Hudhayfah (ibn al Yaman) had three qualities which particularly impressed the Prophet: his unique intelligence, which he employed in dealing with difficult situations; his quick wittedness and spontaneous response to the call for action; and his ability to keep a secret even under persistent questioning.

A noticeable policy of the Prophet was to bring out and use the special qualities and strengths of each of his companions. In deploying his companions, he was careful to choose the right man for the right task. This he did to excellent advantage in the case of Hudhayfah. One of the gravest problems the Muslims of Madinah had to face was the existence of hypocrites (*munafiqun*) in their midst. ... Although many of them had declared their acceptance of Islam, the change was only superficial and they continued to plot and intrigue against the Prophet and the Muslims.

Because of Hudhayfah's ability to keep a secret, the Prophet (*saw*) confided in him the names of the *munafiqin*. It was a weighty secret that the Prophet did not disclose to any of his other companions. He gave Hudhayfah the task of watching the movements of the *munafiqin*, following their activities, and shielding the Muslims from the sinister danger they represented. It was a tremendous responsibility. The *munafiqun*, because they acted in secrecy and because they knew all the developments and plans of the Muslims from within, presented a greater threat to the community than the outright hostility of the *kuffar*.

From this time onwards. Hudhayfah was called "The Keeper of the Secret of the Messenger of Allah." Throughout his life, he remained faithful to his pledge not to disclose the names of the hypocrites. After the death of the Prophet, the *Khalifah* often came to him to seek his advice concerning their movements and activities but he remained tight-lipped and cautious.[97]

---

[97] Hamid, Abul Wahid. (1995). *Companions of the Prophet.* Leicester, UK: MELS, vol. 2, pp. 28–29.

WHAT TYPE OF LEADER ARE YOU?

Directions:

Answer the following questions, keeping in mind what you have done, or think you would do, in situations similar to the ones described.

		Y	N
1.	Do you like the authority which leadership brings?		
2.	Generally, do you think it is worth the time and effort for a leader to explain the reasons for a decision or policy before putting the policy into effect?		
3.	Do you tend to prefer the planning functions of leadership, as opposed to working directly with your members?		
4.	A stranger comes into your work area, and you know the person is a new member. Would you first ask, "What is your name?," rather than introduce yourself?		
5.	Do you keep your members totally up-to-date on developments affecting the group?		
6.	Do you find out that in giving assignments, you tend to state the goals, and leave the methods of performing the tasks up to your members?		
7.	Do you think leaders should remain distant from members, because in the long run familiarity breeds less respect?		
8.	When deciding about an event (e.g., a training camp), you have heard that the majority prefers to have it on Saturday, but you are sure Sunday would be better for all. Would you put the question to a vote rather than make the decision yourself?		
9.	If you could, would you actively seek advice from your members on a person-to-person level?		
10.	Do you find it fairly easy to give low ratings when evaluating your members?		
11.	Do you feel you should be friendly with your members?		
12.	After considerable time, you determine the answer to a tough problem. You pass along the solution to your members who critique it rigorously. Would you be annoyed that the problem is still unsolved, rather than become upset with them?		
13.	Do you agree that one of the best ways to avoid problems of discipline is to provide adequate punishment for violation of rules?		
14.	Your members are criticizing the way you handled a situation. Would you try to convince them, rather than stress that your decisions—as leader—are final?		
15.	Do you generally leave it up to your members to contact you whenever informal day-to-day communications are needed?		
16.	Do you feel that your members should have some personal loyalty to you?		
17.	Do you like using committees, rather than making decisions alone?		
18.	Do you perceive differences of opinion within your work group as being healthy?		

SCORING OF LEADERSHIP QUESTIONNAIRE		
On the scoring matrix below, please place a check mark (✓) next to the question that you answered 'Y'. Add up the checks for each column and put the totals in the appropriate spaces.		
Scoring Matrix		
1.	2.	3.
4.	5.	6
7.	8.	9.
10.	11.	12.
13.	14.	15.
16.	17.	18.
Directive TOTAL =	Participative TOTAL =	Free-rein TOTAL =

Please note that if you receive a high score on both the directive and the participative styles, you have a "team-oriented" style of leadership.

WHAT TYPE OF FOLLOWER ARE YOU?

Directions:

Answer the following questions, keeping in mind what you have done, or think you would do, in the situations similar to the ones described:

		Y	N
1.	When assigned a task, do you like to have the details explained thoroughly?		
2.	Do you think that most leaders are bossier than they need to be?		
3.	Would you say that personal initiative is one of your stronger points?		
4.	Do you feel that a leader should avoid getting becoming too friendly with members?		
5.	In general, do you prefer working with others, instead of working alone?		
6.	Do you prefer the pleasures of solitude (e.g., reading) instead of the pleasures of being with others (e.g., get-togethers)?		
7.	Do you tend to be loyal towards your leader?		
8.	Do you often help others in your work group?		
9.	When you work on a project, do you prefer using your own ideas, instead of your leader's to solve problems?		
10.	Would you prefer a leader who is knowledgeable over one who comes to you to solve problems?		
11.	Do you feel it is appropriate for a leader to be friendlier with some members than with others?		
12.	Would you prefer assuming full responsibility for the outcome, rather than sharing the responsibility with others?		
13.	Do you think that having groups with diverse backgrounds creates more problems than having groups with the same background?		
14.	Do you think a leader should discuss new procedures with his/her members before implementing them?		
15.	Do you insist upon doing what you, yourself, feel is right or important?		
16.	Would you agree that a leader who could not keep your loyalty should not be a leader?		
17.	Would you be upset with a leader who fails to have regular organizational meetings?		
18.	Do rules and prescribed guidelines inhibit your creativity?		

SCORING OF FOLLOWER QUESTIONNAIRE

On the scoring matrix below, please place a check mark (✓) next to the question that you answered 'Y'. Add up the checks for each column and put the totals in the appropriate spaces.

Scoring Matrix

1.	2.	3.
4.	5.	6
7.	8.	9.
10.	11.	12.
13.	14.	15.
16.	17.	18.
Directive TOTAL =	Participative TOTAL =	Free-rein TOTAL =

Please note that if you receive a high score on both the directive and the participative styles, you have a "team-oriented" style of followership.

Chapter 4
Mobilizing, Developing and Organizing Followers

As part of the Ummah, the ultimate role of leaders of Islamic organizations is similar to the role of all of Allah's messengers (as): carrying the message of Islam to mankind.[98]

$$هُوَ ٱلَّذِىٓ أَرْسَلَ رَسُولَهُ بِٱلْهُدَىٰ وَدِينِ ٱلْحَقِّ لِيُظْهِرَهُ$$

$$عَلَى ٱلدِّينِ كُلِّهِ ۦ وَلَوْ كَرِهَ ٱلْمُشْرِكُونَ$$

> It is He who hath sent His messenger with guidance and religion of truth to proclaim it over all religions even though the pagans may detest (it). (Al Taubah, 9:33)

To carry out their role, leaders need to mobilize people because they are both the targets of the message and the channel for transmitting the message.[99] The reason is that leaders cannot and should not be expected to do everything by themselves. The example of the Prophet Muhammad (saw) at the battle of Badr is particularly meaningful. With respect to this momentous victory, Allah pointed out:

$$يَـٰٓأَيُّهَا ٱلنَّبِىُّ حَسْبُكَ ٱللَّهُ وَمَنِ ٱتَّبَعَكَ مِنَ ٱلْمُؤْمِنِينَ$$

> O Apostle! Allah is sufficient for you and for those who follow you of the believers.[100] (Anfaal, 8:64)

---

[98] Maudoodi, pp. 71 and 73.

[99] Murad, talk 4.

[100] Pickthall, Muhammad Marmaduke. *The Meaning of The Glorious Qur'an: Text and Explanatory Translation.* All English translations of the Qur'an used in this book are from

The above *ayat* mentions the two sources of the Muslim army's victory at Badr: Allah's help and a group of believers. Both sources are what every Muslim leader needs to carry forth the message or to fulfill his organization's mission. Allah's help is hoped for and expected if the leader and a critical mass of followers satisfy the moral qualities outlined in Chapter 2 earlier. We will focus here on what a leader needs to do to procure the help of other Muslims.

Mobilizing Followers

Previous chapters described the characteristics that followers should develop in themselves through *tazkiyyah*. Preceding this process is an enlistment phase. Khurram Murad discusses part of the process used by the Prophet (*saw*) in detail,[101] and this process is summarized here:

- **Reach out to everybody.** Just as the message of Islam is nonelitist, being a follower in Islam is not an elitist process. The idea that only a small, selective, and highly trained group of Muslims can energize the remainder of the Ummah is misleading. Both quality and quantity are needed. In spreading the message, a Muslim leader must not ignore anyone. Every single individual, because he is a *khalifa* of Allah, must be made aware of Allah's message. In a famous incident reported in the Qur'an in *Surah 'Abasa* (80:1–3), the Prophet Muhammad (*saw*) was engaged in discussion with a group of Quraishi chieftains. He earnestly wanted to convey the message of Islam to them. While he was thus engaged, Ibn Um Makhtum, a blindman who was very interested in Islam, interrupted the Prophet (*saw*). The Prophet then frowned to express his discontent. Allah rebuked the Prophet for turning away from Ibn Um Makhtum who was already interested in Islam and for focusing instead on a group of nobles who were not as enthusiastic about Islam. As the Prophet (*saw*) learned, every person, regardless of his or her socioeconomic status, requires exposure to the message of Islam.

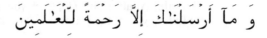

Yusuf Ali. Since the classical English style used by Yusuf Ali may sometimes be difficult to understand, we are at times (as is the case here) using Pickthall's translations. All such instances will be clearly footnoted.

[101] Murad, talk 4.

> We sent you not but as a mercy for all creatures.
> (Anbiyaa, 21:107)

- **The most reticent person may become the best person.** In approaching Muslims (or non-Muslims), one should not prejudge; upon acquiring the "appropriate" knowledge, one may excel in Islam. Hence, someone who was once an enemy of Muslims may be transformed into one of the champions of Islam. The Prophet Muhammad (*saw*) once said:

The best before Islam are the best in Islam if they comprehend (the religious knowledge).[102]

We need only remember the story of 'Umar ibn al Khattab before and after he embraced Islam. Before he embraced Islam, he was very harsh against Muslims, and even plotted to kill the Prophet (*saw*). After he became a Muslim, he participated in all the battles with the Prophet (*saw*), and was one of the few who stood by him during the debacle at Uhud.

- **Accept the verbal commitment of others to Islam at face value.** No Muslim can reject another person's pledge or *shahāda* under any circumstance. The following incident is reported about Usama bin Zaid by himself in *Sahih al Bukhari*, and amply illustrates this approach:

Allah's Messenger sent us toward al Huruqa, and in the morning we attacked them and defeated them. I and an *ansari* man followed a man from among them and when we overtook him, he said, "La ilaha illa Allah." On hearing this, the *ansari* man stopped, but I killed him by stabbing him with my spear. When we returned, the Prophet came to know about what had happened and he said, "O Usama! Did you kill him after he had said "La ilaha illa Allah?" I said, "But he said so only to save himself." The Prophet repeated this so often that I wished I had not embraced Islam before that day.[103]

Zaid's rationale in wishing that he had not embraced Islam before that day stems from the fact that all previous sins of an unbeliever (except for debts) are forgiven by Allah when that person embraces Islam. Had Zaid embraced Islam after the deed described above, he would have been forgiven.

- **Welcome even sinners and try to improve them.** The example of Abdullah bin Ubayy — a person known for deliberately causing

---

[102] Narrated by Abu Hurairah, *Sahih al Bukhari,* hadith 4.593.
[103] Usama Bin Zaid in *Sahih al Bukhari,* 5:568.

dissension among the Prophet's (*saw*) *Muhajir*s and the *Ansars*—
should be kept in mind. In spite of all this person's misdeeds, the
Prophet (*saw*) did not punish him.

- **Repel evil with good:** The Prophet (*saw*) and his Companions were
harassed and subjected to severe hardships by the unbelievers. Allah
enjoined upon them to turn back evil with good deeds:

وَ لَا تَسْتَوِى الْحَسَنَةُ وَ لَا السَّيِّئَةُ ٱدْفَعْ بِالَّتِى هِى

أَحْسَنُ فَإِذَا الَّذِى بَيْنَكَ وَ بَيْنَهُ عَدَاوَةٌ كَأَنَّهُ وَلِىٌّ حَمِيمٌ

> The good deed and the evil deed are not alike. Repel
> the evil deed with one which is better, then lo! he,
> between whom and you there was enmity (will
> become) as though he was a bosom friend.[104]
> (Fussilat, 41:34)

A good deed overpowers a bad deed. Many examples from the life of
the Prophet (*saw*) support this, such as his magnanimous forgiveness
of Hind bint Utbah who had his Uncle Hamzah killed and then ate
from his liver. At her request, Muhammad (*saw*) also forgave her
husband, Abu Sufyan — the leader of enemy forces against the
Muslims.

- **Use an incremental approach.** The Prophet's approach is what
Khurram Murad labels *gradualism.* Just as a plot of new land needs
to be cleared, ploughed, and fertilized before being seeded, a
member needs to be nurtured before being entrusted with major
responsibilities. Bring up progressively, according to his or her
capability, everyone who is attracted to an Islamic organization.
Muslims should not flinch from any responsibility because Allah has
promised them that any test that they go through shall not exceed
their capabilities:

لَا يُكَلِّفُ ٱللَّهُ نَفْسًا إِلَّا وُسْعَهَا لَهَا مَا كَسَبَتْ وَ عَلَيْهَا

مَا ٱكْتَسَبَتْ رَبَّنَا لَا تُؤَاخِذْنَا إِن نَسِينَا أَوْ أَخْطَأْنَا

---

[104] Translation by Pickthall.

رَبَّنَا وَ لا تَحْمِلْ عَلَيْنَآ إِصْرًا كَمَا حَمَلْتَهُ عَلَى ٱلَّذِينَ

مِن قَبْلِنَا رَبَّنَا وَ لا تُحَمِّلْنَا مَالا طَاقَةَ لَنَا بِهِ وَ ٱعْفُ عَنَّا

وَ ٱغْفِرْ لَنَا وَ ٱرْحَمْنَآ أَنتَ مَوْلَـٰنَا فَٱنصُرْنَا عَلَى

ٱلْقَوْمِ ٱلْكَـٰفِرِينَ   ❖❖

> On no soul does Allah place a burden greater than it
> can bear. It gets every good that it earns and it
> suffers every ill that it earns. (Pray): "Our Lord!
> condemn us not if we forget or fall into error; Our
> Lord! Lay not on us a burden like that which You
> did lay on those before us; Our Lord! lay not on us a
> burden greater than we have strength to bear. Blot
> out our sins and grant us forgiveness. Have mercy
> on us. You are our Protector; help us against those
> who stand against faith." (Al Baqarah, 2:286)

In the case of a member whose knowledge and practice of Islam is
somewhat weak, you may wish to follow the incremental approach
recommended by Allah — encourage him or her to adopt *taqwa* as
much as he or she is able to.

فَٱتَّقُوا اللَّهَ مَاٱسْتَطَعْتُمْ وَٱسْمَعُوا وَ أَطِيعُوا وَ أَنفِقُوا خَيْرًا

لَّأَنفُسِكُمْ وَمَن يُوقَ شُحَّ نَفْسِهِ فَأُولَـٰئِكَ هُمُ الْمُفْلِحُونَ

> So fear Allah as much as you can; listen and obey;
> and spend in charity for the benefit of your own
> souls: and those saved from the covetousness of
> their own souls they are the ones that achieve
> prosperity. (Al Taghabun, 64:16)

After all, we have the example that the commands about alcohol
drinking became progressively more prohibitive. If gradualism can
be used by Allah and His Prophet (*saw*) to transform his *Sahaba* who
had been sunk in *jahiliyyah* before Islam, so too it can be adopted by
contemporary Islamic leaders.

- **Allocate assignments according to each person's capability.**
  During the time of the Prophet (*saw*), bedouins tended to be
  uneducated people, accustomed to a very simple way of life. The
  following hadith demonstrates his ability to transmit the core
  message of Islam according to his audience's frame of reference:

  A bedouin came to the Prophet and said, "Tell me of such a deed as will
  make me enter Paradise if I do it." The Prophet (*saw*) said, "Worship Allah,
  and worship none along with Him, offer the (five) prescribed compulsory
  prayers perfectly, pay the compulsory zakat, and fast the month of
  Ramadan." The Bedouin said, "By Him, in whose hands my life is, I will not
  do more than this." When he (the bedouin) left, the Prophet said, "Whoever
  likes to see a man of Paradise, then he may look at this man." [105]

  On the other hand, when the Prophet (*saw*) dealt with companions
  who had higher responsibilities and a deeper understanding of Islam,
  he would ask more from them. For example, at the time of the
  hijrah, he asked Ali (*ra*) to stay behind in order to repay some things
  entrusted to and deposited with the Prophet (*saw*). 'Ali stayed in
  spite of the fact that the Prophet's house was surrounded and
  watched by an armed group of would-be assassins. Later, he was the
  standard bearer specially appointed by the Prophet (*saw*) on the
  critical day of Khaybar.[106]

- **Exhibit patience and understanding.** Sometimes, a member may
  slip. Rather than criticizing him, be patient and understanding. The
  following verse from the Qur'an revealed after the near debacle at
  Uhud illustrates this point vividly:

فَبِمَا رَحْمَةٍ مِّنَ ٱللَّهِ لِنتَ لَهُمْ وَلَوْ كُنتَ فَظًّا غَلِيظَ

ٱلْقَلْبِ لَٱنفَضُّواْ مِنْ حَوْلِكَ فَٱعْفُ عَنْهُمْ وَٱسْتَغْفِرْ لَهُمْ

وَشَاوِرْهُمْ فِى ٱلْأَمْرِ فَإِذَا عَزَمْتَ فَتَوَكَّلْ عَلَى ٱللَّهِ إِنَّ

ٱللَّهَ يُحِبُّ ٱلْمُتَوَكِّلِينَ

> It is part of the mercy of Allah that you do deal
> gently with them. Were you severe or harsh-hearted

---

[105] Narrated by Abu Hurairah, *Sahih Bukhari*, 2.480.

[106] As-Suyuti, Jalal ad-Din (1996). *The History of The Khalifahs Who Took the Right
Way*. Translation of *Tarikh al Khulafa* by 'Abdassamad Clarke. London: Ta-Ha Publishers,
p. 174.

> they would have broken away from about you; so
> pass over (their faults) and ask for (Allah's)
> forgiveness for them; and consult them in affairs (of
> moment). Then when you have taken a decision put
> your trust in Allah. For Allah loves those who put
> their trust (in Him). (Al 'Imran, 3:159)

The above verse was revealed during one of the darkest moments of Islamic history. It came at a time when the Muslim army came very close to defeat because some of the *Sahaba* did not follow the Prophet's explicit instructions. After the battle, Allah instructed His Prophet (*saw*) to overlook this incident, to show patience with his followers, and to continue to work and consult with them. Just because they did not listen to him once did not mean that they were to be set aside; on the contrary, the Prophet was to demonstrate understanding and gentleness.

Developing Followers

Everybody is to be welcome. But because followers or organizational members are not all the same, leaders need to adjust their leadership style to deal with various types of followers in various types of situations. According to research, a leader can shift between any of four leadership styles: directive, coaching, supportive, and delegating, depending upon the maturity of his or her followers. *Maturity* consists of religious maturity (knowledge, understanding, and application of the *dīn*), job maturity (technical knowledge and task-relevant skills), and psychological maturity (personality, self-confidence and self-respect).[107] See Figure 4-1.

Figure 4-1: Situational Leadership Model[108]

Supportive Behavior		Supportive Style	Coaching Style
	High		
		Delegating Style	Directive Style
	Low		
		Mature	Immature

Maturity of Followers

A leader should use a **directive** style when dealing with immature members and when supportive behavior is not needed. A directive style

---

[107] Adapted from Hersey and Blanchard's definition of maturity.
[108] Hersey and Blanchard, p. 188.

involves providing clear and explicit guidelines, and the leader controls the decision-making process. A directive style may also be used in an emergency or life-threatening situation. Ohio State researchers have found that US Air Force crews preferred their commanders to use a task-oriented, directive style instead of a supporting style.[109] Thus, if the organization is experiencing factional trouble, the leader may use a directive style if negotiations between the parties concerned fail repeatedly.

As members learn their tasks and increase in maturity, the leader may wish to shift to a **coaching** style. A coaching style is characterized by two-way communication and an increasing amount of supportive behavior. This type of behavior is needed in order to build confidence in the followers and to motivate them further. The role of the leader as coach will be discussed in more detail later in Chapter Five. After members have built enough self-confidence in performing certain tasks, the leader may now engage in *shura* with respect to these particular tasks, and use a **supportive** style. This style encourages shared decision making, and active two-way communication. A leader using this style aims to support mature employees in the use of their skills.

In a situation where members are mature as well as competent and self-motivated, a leader should use a **delegating** style. Although problem identification may still be done by the leader, he now allows members the responsibility for implementing objectives and permits them to decide how, when, and where to carry out their tasks. Chapter Six will describe in detail how a Muslim leader can delegate effectively.

The situational leadership model suggests that leaders should adjust their leadership style to fit the situation and their followers. Thus, leadership is viewed as an open and dynamic process. The Prophet Muhammad (saw) provides the most excellent example of leadership. As shown above, he adjusted his leadership style depending on the situation: he was directive at Uhud; he used a coaching style with Abu Dharr; he used a supportive style with Salman Al Farsi; and he used a delegating style with Abu Bakr.

Several factors, however, need to be kept in mind when applying the above model. First, can a leader adjust flexibly from one situation to another? Personality research[110] suggests that the personality of followers may not be easily modified, and that to attempt to do so may

---

[109] Stoner, James (1978). *Management.* Englewood Cliffs, NJ: Prentice-Hall, p. 441.

[110] Personality is defined here as 'the stable set of characteristics and tendencies that determine commonalities and differences in people's behavior'.

result in frustration on the part of the leader.[111] Let us assume that you are in charge of a brother Muslim whose skills and leadership style do not fit his current task. You will first want to coach him into improving his skills and adjusting his own leadership style. If this proves impossible, then you will want to move him to another task that better fits his current skills and leadership style, rather than letting him feel helpless. Change the situation to fit the leader if you cannot change the leader to fit the situation.

Second, what should the leader do if his followers vary in maturity? Assuming that the leader can flexibly adjust his style in the same way that the Prophet (*saw*) or Abu Bakr (*ra*) was able to, then he should use different styles of leadership depending on the follower's degree of maturity and the situation he is in.

Third, what about the nature of the task? If the task is complex and it is an emergency, the leader may have to use more of a directive and less of a delegating style. However, should time be adequate, the leader may wish to use any of the other three styles depending again on the level of maturity of his or her followers. He may even use all three styles simultaneously depending on the follower(s).

Once you have mobilized your followers and are using the appropriate style of leadership to facilitate their growth and development into active Islamic workers, then the question becomes: For what are you preparing them? In the rest of this chapter, we describe how you can organize your members who have volunteered to help out.

Organizing Your Followers

To organize his or her followers effectively, an Islamic leader may wish to proceed as follows: [112]

1. Clearly articulate the vision and mission of your organization.[113]

The vision is a compelling, idealized statement of what your organization wishes to become in the future. A vision provides motivation and direction to the efforts of you and your members. The strategic plan of the Muslim Students' Association (MSA) of the United

---

[111] Gibson, J. L., Ivancevich, J. M. and Donnelly, J. H. (1994). *Organizations: Behavior, Structure And Processes*. Burr Ridge, IL: Irwin, p. 134.

[112] Kouzes and Posner (1995).

[113] For a more complete coverage of vision and mission, please visit the Islamic Management Net website at http://www.islamist.org and view the transparencies on the strategic management process.

States and Canada provides us with an excellent example of what an effective vision should look like:

> *To be the medium through which Islam will be the active and progressive force on University and College Campuses throughout North America.*

The mission is a statement describing what the organization wishes to do now to make the vision happen; it also indicates what service you are providing, for whom you are providing it, and how distinctive your service is. Remember, *there is no perfect mission statement*, and you will always be refining it. Some mission statements also include a statement of purpose. An example of an excellent mission statement is that of the Indian Muslim Relief Committee (IMRC) of the Islamic Society of North America.

> *To help India's Muslims achieve security, freedom, and equality — their rights as citizens of India.*

The above vision and mission statements have been used quite effectively by the leadership of both the MSA and IMRC to energize and channel the efforts of their membership. To enact the organization's vision and mission, organizational members must be galvanized into volunteering for its different activities and programs.

2. Develop a statement of your organization's philosophy regarding volunteer services.

Based on the above vision and mission statements, you need to develop a statement that explains to the volunteers what their contribution will be toward fulfilling the mission, and what they will receive in return. This statement will serve as the foundation for organizing the volunteers' efforts and designing roles that will specify exactly what they are expected to do. Here is a sample statement regarding your organization's philosophy with respect to volunteer services:

This organization's drug prevention volunteer program provides you with quality involvement in the delivery of drug prevention services to the community based on the following beliefs:

- Volunteers, by their educational expertise, professional training and past experience, can provide unique professional and realistic advice to potential drug users.

- Volunteers expand the organization's resource base, and allow us to help more of the targeted sector of the community than paid staff working alone.

- Volunteers are the organization's representatives in the community.

- Volunteers provide the organization with direct feedback about the needs of potential drug users and how to help them better.

- Volunteers, by nurturing potential and current drug users away from un-Islamic practices, will be engaging in a process of *tazkiyyah*, and will experience personal growth as Muslims.

3. Develop volunteer positions.

As you develop your membership, it is important to give them tasks that will further cement their involvement in your organization. You cannot just assign tasks to people without an overall plan. The three steps outlined above provide you with a good foundation. Now, you will need to develop a set of volunteer positions based around the services that your organization aims to provide. To do so, you may wish to ask yourself the following questions:[114]

- What are the characteristics and needs of the target population?
- What are the qualifications required of the volunteers needed to serve the target population?
- How do the proposed volunteer positions relate to your organization's staff?
- What activities will the volunteers be responsible for, and what benefits will they receive from these activities?
- How can the volunteers be involved in the overall design of their respective tasks?
- How can the volunteer be encouraged to take responsibility for the results of his or her own task? How will these results be measured and communicated back to the organization?

Here is an example of a position description[115] for a volunteer for the drug program:

---

[114] Fisher, J. and Cole, K. (1993). *Leadership and Management of Volunteer Programs.* San Francisco: Jossey-Bass, Chapter 2.

[115] Based on a sample position guide described in Fisher and Cole (1993).

Sample Job Description for a Volunteer

Job Title:	Youth Counselor
Program Mission:	To assist parents by explaining to their children (between the ages of eight and sixteen) about drugs and the need to stay drug free.
Goals:	Develop a nurturing relationship with four children who are at risk. Assess and build on the children's strengths. Facilitate the children's personal growth by improving their self-esteem and identification with Islam and Muslim role models.
Responsibilities:	Visit assigned children one hour a week. Work with organization's professional social worker, and map children's weekly progress. Participate in monthly discussion with social worker and other volunteers in the same position.
Qualifications:	At least 20 years of age. Practicing Muslim. Skilled in interpersonal relationships. Good judgment.
Training:	Initial weekend training program with the social worker, and a two-month mentoring program with an experienced youth counselor.
Performance Appraisal:	Quarterly meeting (every three months) with social worker to assess progress of children.
Benefits:	Tazkiyyah resulting from serving as a helping brother or sister to children at risk. Opportunity to work with a professional social worker and to earn credit towards psychology course at the local university.

4. Do not go overboard by creating a multitude of tasks.

Parsimony is critical in designing the tasks for your volunteer. Keep the tasks realistic and achievable, and always make sure to involve the volunteer in planning, organizing, and evaluating his or her own task.

Begin from what is possible. As indicated by Khan,[116] this principle stems from a hadith reported by Aisha (*ra*) in which she said:

> Whenever Allah's Apostle was given the choice of one of two matters, he would choose the easier of the two, as long as it was not sinful to do so, but if it was sinful to do so, he would not approach it. [117]

The first step toward a goal is the most important one. To the extent that one starts from the possible, one is, *insha' Allah*, more likely to reach one's goal.

5. Reward both process and outcome.

If volunteers perform well at their own tasks, reward them. Reward them too for trying, even if they do not meet the predefined targets on their first tries. This approach to process improvement is clearly recognized in Islam.

> Allah ordered (the appointed angels over you) that the good and the bad deeds be written, and He then showed (the way) how (to write). If someone intends to do a good deed and he does not do it, Allah writes for him a full good deed (in his account with Him); and if he intends to do a good deed and actually does it, then Allah writes for him (in his account) from ten to seven hundred times or more its equal as a reward. If someone intends to do a bad deed and he does not do it, Allah writes a full good deed (in his account); and if he intends to do it (a bad deed) and actually does it, Allah writes one bad deed (in his account).[118]

Rather than merely looking at the number of times a volunteer achieves his or her target, recognize the efforts of someone who may be trying very hard, but who may not have achieved much yet. For example, a volunteer may work extremely hard at drug counseling, but may not succeed because he or she is dealing with repeat offenders who simply do not care.

6. Develop a nurturing Islamic organizational climate.

All of the above should be molded into a climate in which Islamic values act as an umbrella for the activities of all organization members (and volunteers) including yours. Your organization exists to serve Allah; all of its activities should be directed toward that sole purpose as expressed by your vision and mission statements. Transform your

---

[116] Khan, Muhammad W. (1998). "Prophetic Principles of Success." *Minaret*, September issue, pp. 8–9.

[117] Narrated by Aisha (*ra*), *Sahih al Bukhari*, Hadith 4.760.

[118] Narrated by Ibn Abbas (*ra*), *Sahih al Bukhari*, Hadith 8.498.

organization into one in which learning and *tazkiyyah* are an integral part of its culture. Within the parameters of Islam, encourage your volunteers to engage in planned and self-initiated activities. A combination of both will give them a sense of direction and challenge as they try their best *fi sabil lillah* (for Allah's sake).

Chapter 5

The Leader as Coach or Mentor

An effective leader needs to develop the members for whom he is responsible. By helping them to enhance their skills, he can derive two important benefits.[119] First, he can delegate and gain more time to expand his own capabilities. Second, he can create a lasting source of effective followers and future leaders. Although most organizations recognize the importance of coaching, few do well in this area.

What Is Coaching?

Coaching is neither career counseling nor performance appraisal. Although it includes both of these activities, it is "a day-to-day, hands-on process of helping employees to recognize opportunities that improve their performance and capabilities."[120] Coaching requires a leader to provide more than on-the-job training: He must be able to assess carefully ways to raise members' performance and skills, outline mutually acceptable goals, build a supportive climate and influence them to improve their behavior.

The Role of Coaching

An effective leader's job includes three distinct roles: manager, evaluator, and coach. As a manager, he is responsible for outlining and communicating performance goals. He may say the following to his new fundraising committee chairperson, "Based on the current income level of the community and our mosque's projected building costs, I want you

---

[119] Wilkinson, H. (1993). *Influencing People in Organizations*. Fort Worth, TX: The Dryden Press, pp. 105–113.

[120] Ibid., p. 106.

to raise $25,000 by the end of December, God willing." As an evaluator, he must conduct periodic performance appraisals. In March, May, July, September, and November, he may have a meeting with the fundraising chairperson to go over fundraising activities, collections, and pledges. As a coach, he is expected to assist organizational members on a day-to-day basis as well as over the long term. Specifically, he must help them identify and improve key skills.

Of the three roles mentioned above, coaching is the most difficult. Why? In general, performance is a function of the interaction between capabilities and motivation. Unless a leader helps a brother or sister improve his or her capabilities, performance will be low even if the brother or sister is highly motivated. Conversely, being highly skilled does not ensure a high degree of motivation on the part of the member. For members to desire to improve their capabilities and better their performance, they need to know that efforts in these directions are expected, and that change will be nonthreatening and in their ultimate best interests. Hence, a key element of coaching is the development of a set of expectations between leader and member. These expectations can, in turn, be defined more explicitly as performance goals, thus allowing the mentor to observe on-the-job performance and to give exact feedback. Given the dynamic environment in which most organizations function, the leader must remember to renegotiate expectations as often as necessary. Adjusting expectations too frequently, however, may disorient the member and undermine his confidence in his capabilities.

Creating the proper climate

Both the organization's climate and the behavior of the leader need to be fine-tuned simultaneously when the leader functions either as an evaluator or as a coach.

- As an evaluator, a leader judges an organization member's performance against previously agreed upon goals and objectives.

- As a coach, a leader postpones judgment, listens empathetically, probes for concerns related to the employee's self-assessment, and is ready to offer specific suggestions regarding training and self-development opportunities.

For the coaching process to work, the leader must build a positive climate; he must facilitate the free and open flow of ideas. The member must view this climate as a nurturing one. Here are some tips on how to create such an environment:

- Never threaten by words or by action. Avoid statements such as "If you do not straighten up, you will be replaced." Threats and unwarranted use of coercive power usually make brothers or sisters become defensive, angry, or may actually lead them to drop out of the organization. After all, they are volunteers, and have a choice.

- The mentor and member must have an understanding relationship. The member should respect the mentor's integrity and capacity as leader, and the mentor should respect the member's integrity and capacity to do the job.

- The coaching session must not be interrupted by distractions. Very often, a leader will be coaching during lunch or in the parking lot. Set aside uninterrupted blocks of time when you will coach a member.

- Timing affects coaching sessions. After a critical presentation to the board of trustees, a brother or sister may be elated or upset. Wait until he or she is ready to listen to feedback. At the same time, delaying too long may cause him or her to forget events.

- While being coached, a member must understand that his or her leader is acting as a coach, not as an evaluator. Hence, the member should perceive his leader as supportive rather than critical.

- Remember that as a Muslim coach, you need to make sure that Islamic behavior is observed when mentoring members of the opposite sex. Always be in an open, public location to avoid potential problems.

Five Critical Skills

All leaders need training in coaching. There are five key skills that managers need in preparing to be a coach.

1. Observational skills

Mentors should keep track of their members' performances on a day-to-day basis, so as to spot opportunities for members to expand their capabilities. Once they identify relevant opportunities, they must act immediately. To the extent that members associate their immediate behaviors with their leader/mentor's observations, they will be more likely to make amends and improve their performance in the future. In gathering information, leaders may obtain data via direct observation, or their networks of relationships with other members.

2. Analytical skills

Leaders must be able to recognize development opportunities for their members, and they must determine whether and when coaching is needed to take full advantage of these opportunities. Identifying such opportunities depends on the information gathered through direct observations and through indirect data obtained from other sources. In addition, leaders should talk with members to ascertain the validity of their data. Overall, a mentor will need the answer to several of the following questions before providing feedback and advice to a member:

- How did he or she perform the task?
- What was done properly?
- What areas need to be worked on?
- What other procedures or techniques might he or she use?
- What specific alternatives can the member try to improve himself and his performance?

The purpose of this step is not to label or embarrass the member but rather to establish *where* the member is at. What is his or her real potential? A superficial understanding of a member is potentially dangerous to both the leader and the member. If the members receive poor advice, they may become discouraged, and keep away from the *jamā'a*. If the leader is identified as a poor coach, his or her own credibility and effectiveness will suffer. The leader should probe patiently until he or she has carefully assessed what is *really* going on, and how best to help the member. To avoid any potential negative reaction from members being coached, proceed incrementally, rather than in quantum leaps.

3. Delegating skills

Delegation is the process by which a leader assigns to his members the right to act and to make decisions in certain areas.[121] Delegation is an important leadership skill that should be developed. It enables the leader to give others a chance to develop themselves. It also motivates them because of the enhanced sense of responsibility that it provides. Finally, in situations where the follower is separated by a large geographical distance from the leader, delegation becomes even more critical because the leader cannot be present.

---

[121] Hellriegel and Slocum, p. G-3.

Delegating involves three components:[122]

- a task,
- some degree of authority or power, and
- responsibility.

Delegation starts when leaders divide the tasks that need to be performed in order to achieve a certain goal. In delegating, leaders should select their delegates carefully, and grant them an amount of authority equal to the responsibilities being allocated. Leaders should remember, however, that they may delegate away some authority or power, but that they are ultimately accountable for the results of any tasks assigned to their members. In other words, *delegate, do not abdicate.* Simultaneously, the leader needs to explain to the delegates both the scope and nature of their tasks. Progress checks are still required, and specific, mutually agreeable time limits need to be set. A leader's ability to delegate effectively is one of the more critical skills that must be developed. The next chapter will explore this particular skill in detail.

4. Interviewing skills

Leaders need to develop their skills as interviewers by asking appropriate questions and by listening attentively. Three types of questions can be asked in performing this task:

1. *Open-ended questions that lead members to reconsider their problems.* Do not say, "What you did will never work. Do as I do." Instead, ask the member, "What other strategies have you looked at?" or "What may or may not work with your strategy?" or "What have other members tried in similar situations?"
2. *Closed questions that help the leader to focus on a specific area.* For example, ask, "Who in the organization is responsible for processing membership applications?"
3. *Reflective questions that repeat a statement the person has made for the purpose of clarification.* If a brother were to say, "Sister Aafia is uncooperative," an effective coach may ask, "Does she refuse to work on a specific project, all projects, or only on projects that you are in charge of?"

While interviewing a member, a leader should remember the importance of listening. Develop *active* listening skills. Keep quiet and listen; if you keep interrupting the member or find yourself using the

---

[122] Wilkinson, p. 83–85.

word "but," you may not be listening at all. Also avoid selective listening: hearing what you wish to hear while filtering out any data that does not fit your preconceived ideas. Use appropriate body language such as nods to elicit more information. Active listening does *not* mean breaking the Islamic etiquette of modesty when communicating with a person of the opposite sex!

5. Feedback skills

If a member becomes defensive or angry, the leader has not provided effective feedback. Ineffective feedback may not help the member improve his behavior. Here are some guidelines[123] for improving a leader's feedback skills:

- *Be specific, not general.* Telling a member that he or she was unwise is not helpful. Provide details. For example, say, "Salim was not happy when he heard your latest directives. How can you develop a more positive relationship with him?" The Prophet (*saw*) was very direct (but diplomatic) in giving feedback. In a hadith reported by Abu Dharr, he asked the Prophet (*saw*) to be appointed to a public office. The Prophet (*saw*)' responded by stroking his shoulder and saying, "Abu Dharr, you are weak, and authority is a trust."[124] The direct feedback was preceded by a shoulder stroke so that Abu Dharr would not feel hurt.

- *Be descriptive, not evaluative.* Telling someone that he or she was unwise is not helpful. By so doing, the leader is not acting as a coach; he is being judgmental. Instead, the leader should say, "When you prepared the conference's schedule, you might have looked at how much time you were providing the audience between sessions."

- *Take both your own and your member's needs into account.* Do not give feedback when angry or under the influence of other powerful emotions, such as sorrow. At such moments, a leader may lose objectivity and may hurt a member's feelings.

- *Be sure feedback addresses behavior that can be modified.* If the member has no *control* over a certain obstacle, the leader will only increase the member's sense of powerlessness and frustration. If a member is given a task that requires the coordinated efforts of more

---

[123] Ibid., p. 111.
[124] *Sahih Muslim,* vol, 3, p. 1015.

than one person, any comment about increasing performance efficiency may be misplaced.

- *Be sure feedback is private.* Unless the feedback is being directed to a group, do not give feedback in front of others. Nobody likes to be critiqued in public.

- *Be sure feedback is well timed.* Give feedback immediately unless a time out is needed for either the member or the leader in order for emotions to simmer down. If the member has just failed a major exam, the last thing he wants to hear about is his or her poor bookkeeping skills.

- *Use multiple channels.* Communicate via multiple channels of communication, and communicate directly in order to ensure that you and the member have clearly understood each other. Do not just have a five-minute conversation; reconfirm via the telephone or a short note soon thereafter.

The importance of providing feedback in an open and opportune manner is illustrated in the following exchange between Abu Bakr (*ra*) and Khalid ibn Walid (*ra*). Khalid had been sent to discipline a tribal chief, Muja'ah. Upon learning that Khalid had married the daughter of this tribal chief, Abu Bakr did not immediately act to discipline his army's commander. Instead, he wrote to him, asking him to explain his behavior:

> O Khalid! ... You are enjoying yourself with your bride, while the blood of twelve hundred Muslims (which was spilled in the battle) right at your doorstep has not dried yet. Muja'ah was able to deceive you and entice you to a treaty after you had defeated his people.[125]

Upon receiving this message, Khalid responded as follows:

> I assure you that I did not take my bride until I was satisfied (with the results of the battle) and my mission was completed. And I have chosen to marry (the daughter of a person) whom I would travel from Madina to seek his relation, but my engagement to his (daughter) was prompted as I am present here. If you disapprove of my marriage for (any) temporal or religious (reasons), I will desist.[126]

This exchange between Abu Bakr (*ra*) and Khalid (*ra*) illustrates how feedback can be used to clarify misgivings and dispel suspicions in potentially explosive situations. Such feedback must be coupled with a

---

[125] 'Arjun, *Khalid ibn al Walid*, 201 as cited in Safi, 218.
[126] Ibid.

genuine desire for fairness and a concern for the well-being and development of followers.

Stages of Coaching

The coaching relationship between a leader and his or her members evolves over time. Empirical research on coaching has revealed that there are four stages to this process:[127]

1. *Initiation,* which is the period when the coaching relationship begins. It lasts between six to twelve months. During this time, the leader sets expectations, coachs, and provides challenging tasks. In return, the member works on achieving the set goals, and exhibits a desire to be coached.
2. *Cultivation,* which is the period that lasts between two to five years. During this period, interaction is frequent, and work is on a broad spectrum of increasingly more meaningful and challenging tasks. The emotional bond between the leader and his or her member deepens.
3. *Separation,* which lasts between six months to two years. At this stage, the member wants the opportunity to work on his or her own, and the leader will delegate more and more, being available only for consultation during crises.
4. *Redefinition,* which is an indefinite period following the separation phase. The coaching relationship is discarded, and a peer relationship develops between the leader and the member.

Overall, the coaching process is *not* a one-day event. Lasting relationships between a leader and his or her members take time to nurture, but members must be cut loose at the appropriate time. *Insha' Allah,* the coaching relationship will then evolve into an enduring bond.

Coaching as *Tarbiyyah* and Self-Development

Just as the objective of *wudhu* is not *wudhu* itself but rather *salat* and submission to Allah's will, so the objective of coaching as *tarbiyyah*[128] (training) is not coaching in itself. Ultimately, coaching should focus on the self-development of the individual as a Muslim. The coach can only

---

[127] Kram, K. E. (1983). "Phases of the Mentor Relationship." *Academy of Management Journal.* December, p. 622.

[128] Based partly on Khurram Murad's lecture on self-development, cassette no. 7.

provide instructional or role-modeling help, but the primary responsibility for the outcome of the coaching process rests on the individual being coached. An analogy from nature may be useful here: The beneficial aspects of rain can only work when it falls on fertile soil. When it falls on a sheet of rock, it just washes away. Coaching is comparable to rain — to the extent that the member is receptive to the coach, he or she will benefit from it and act Islamically on his or her own; however, to the extent that the member rejects the coach's efforts, nothing will result from this interaction.

When coaching a member toward self-development, the coach must follow a few basic principles:

1. Start every coaching meeting with a short *du'a*, asking Allah for guidance. This *du'a* takes only a minute or two, but places both the coach and the member in the right frame of mind and soul.

2. Do not scare trainees away from Islam by asking them to do difficult things. Anas bin Malik reports that the Prophet (*saw*) once said:

    Facilitate things for people (concerning religious matters), and do not make it hard for them, and give them good tidings and do not make them run away (from Islam).[129]

    As Kouzes and Posner point out, one of the key ingredients in leadership effectiveness is "planning small wins." Make the initial training steps easy for the member so that he can succeed and not be daunted by the task. Do not overreach or ask the member to perform tasks that are beyond his or her control.

3. Remind members that Allah is on their side, and wants them to succeed. He does not want Satan to gain the upperhand:

$$\text{مَّا يَفْعَلُ ٱللَّهُ بِعَذَابِكُمْ إِن شَكَرْتُمْ وَءَامَنتُمْ وَكَانَ}$$
$$\text{ٱللَّهُ شَاكِرًا عَلِيمًا}$$

> What can Allah gain by your punishment if you are grateful and you believe? Nay, it is Allah that recognizes (all good) and knows all things. (Al Nisā', 4:147)

---

[129] *Sahih al Bukhari*, vol. 1, hadith no. 69.

4. Encourage members to have the right intention or *niyat* before engaging in anything. Here 'Umar bin al Khattab reports that the Prophet Muhammad (*saw*) said:

    The reward of deeds depends upon the intentions and every person will get the reward according to what he has intended. So whoever emigrated for worldly benefits or for a woman to marry, his emigration was for what he emigrated for.[130]

5. Urge members to act upon their intention with the understanding that *halal* intentions and efforts will be rewarded by Allah even if the ultimate outcome is not achieved. Thus, one may intend to concentrate during prayer, but find oneself distracted in spite of one's intentions and efforts. Allah rewards people for their intentions and efforts, even if they actually do not succeed completely. In a previously cited verse (Al Baqarah, 2:286), Allah emphasizes this point.

6. Remind members that the aim of self-development is not perfection. No one is perfect except Allah. People who think they have attained perfection are engaging in self-congratulatory arrogance and deluding themselves.

7. Prevent members from getting discouraged. During the process of coaching, members may give up at times because they seem to have reached a stalemate. They need to focus, remembering the plight of the Prophet Yaqub[131] (*as*) in the Qur'an, and how he dealt with the most difficult of situations:

$$\text{يَٰبَنِىَّ اذْهَبُواْ فَتَحَسَّسُواْ مِن يُوسُفَ وَ أَخِيهِ وَ لَا}$$

$$\text{تَايْئَسُواْ مِن رَّوْحِ اللَّهِ إِنَّهُ لَا يَايْئَسُ مِن رَّوْحِ اللَّهِ إِلَّا}$$

$$\text{الْقَوْمُ الْكَٰفِرُونَ}$$

> O my sons! go and enquire about Yusuf and his brother and never give up hope of Allah's soothing mercy: truly no one despairs of Allah's soothing mercy except those who have no faith. (Yusuf, 12:87)

---

[130] *Sahih Bukhari*, vol. 1, hadith no. 1
[131] Yaqub (*as*) is the Arabic name of the Prophet Jacob (*as*).

8. Emphasize that the time for self-development is finite, and that they must manage their time wisely even as they try to better themselves. On the Day of Judgment, everyone will have to account for the use of the time allotted to them during their lives. Therefore, the mentor or coach must try to improve or make progress as diligently and as earnestly as possible.

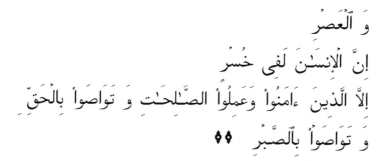

By (the token of) time (through the ages), verily man is in loss except such as have faith and do righteous deeds and (join together) in the mutual teaching of truth and of patience and constancy. (Al 'Asr, 103)

Case Exercise: Islamic Publications Corporation[132]

Islamic Publications Corporation (IPC) is a small publishing house and bookstore located south of Austin, Texas. It prepares and publishes Islamic books for a wide range of audiences, and it markets both these books as well as publications imported from foreign countries. Recently, IPC hired two managers in an effort to expand its operations.

Cassam Sheik had enlisted in the army after finishing high school, and remained there for seven years, rising to the rank of sergeant. At the same time, he converted to Islam. Seeking a career change, he then enrolled in a local community college and earned an associate degree in management. He was hired as bookstore manager at IPC because the president, Khalid Walid, was impressed by his Islamic character and by his experience.

The jobs Cassam supervised were routine and repetitive, consisting mostly of responding to requests for book orders, receiving books from the publishers, monitoring inventory and issuing reports of book sales. These jobs could be learned in a few days. Despite the routine nature of their duties, the brothers and sisters in the bookstore performed well and exhibited little turnover and absenteeism. Based on his army experience, Cassam made a conscious effort to remain distant from his workers and not to become too friendly with them. To impress Br. Khalid, Cassam monitored productivity carefully and spent most of his time observing his workers; he even timed how long it took them to go and come back from prayers. He also gave them a lot of unsolicited advice. In the months following Cassam's hiring, book orders were misplaced, several brothers and sisters resigned, and absenteeism increased. Several bookstore workers were heard mumbling, "I wish he'd stayed in the Army. Where does he think he is?"

At the other end of the IPC complex, Dr. Farida Ibrahim was appointed as head of the publishing house. This section consisted of fifteen full-time and part-time reviewers who were specialists in key areas of Islamic studies. The staff received a flood of manuscripts from numerous countries both because of IPC's reputation, and because of the higher royalties paid to authors. Usually, a manuscript was looked at by at least four reviewers. After the review process, recommendations were then passed on to Ibrahim for her final approval. The review process was

---

[132] The names of this company and all persons mentioned in the above case are fictitious. Any resemblance to any actual organization or living person is purely coincidental.

challenging, although the criteria for differentiating a good manuscript from a bad one were often vague. Dr. Ibrahim had been hired from her position as chair of the Department of Islamic Studies at Temple University. Her management skills as department chair had convinced Br. Khalid that she was the right person to head the publishing house section.

Quickly, Ibrahim decided that she could run the publishing house the way she had run her university department. First, she got to know all her reviewers on a personal basis and assured them that they could come to her if they had problems. She insisted that they were all professional equals. Then, she retired to her office, where she spent most of her time reading Islamic journals and writing articles. "After all," she thought, "these brothers and sisters have advanced degrees. They know what to do." During the next several months, two of Ibrahim's reviewers resigned. Frequent quarrels broke out about who was supposed to review what and when. Worst of all, Ibrahim discovered that two reviewers had incurred a backlog of 15 manuscripts, and were not in a mood to be hurried.

Questions

1.   Why weren't Cassam and Ibrahim effective?

2.   What would you do if you were Cassam or Ibrahim?

Chapter 6
Leadership and Delegation

One of the most important characteristics of effective leadership is the ability to delegate. So, what is delegation? It is a process whereby a leader loans, or transfers, part of his authority to a follower in order to get a task done. It consists of several major steps:[133]

- Assigning to a delegate part of an objective or task, and the responsibility associated with performing that task fully. The delegate must be capable of performing this objective or task.

- Explaining to the delegate what the task consists of, and the rationale behind the task. Although the leader may still be around to provide some measure of support, he or she will seldom tell the delegate how to perform the task. Time constraints are to be explicitly stated, or agreed upon.

- The delegate accepts the responsibility, and begins the task, aware that he is accountable for his performance.

- The leader evaluates the delegate's performance, and may or may not withdraw his support. Should the delegate consistently underperform in spite of repeated feedback, the leader may move him or her to a different position or responsibility.

Assess your delegation skills: please turn to the end of this chapter, and answer the delegation questionnaire. Then go to the page after, and evaluate yourself.

---

[133] Nathaniel Stewart as cited in Steinmetz, Lawrence L. (1976). *The Art and Skill of Delegation.* Reading, MA: Addison-Wesley, p. 4.

The process of delegation and its inherent advantages have been recognized from early on.[134]   When the Prophet Musa (*saw*) was involved in a variety of organizational issues, he went up to his father-in-law who advised him as follows:

> The thing that you do is not good. You will surely wear away ... for these things are too heavy for you. You are not able to perform it yourself alone ... You will provide out of all the people able men ... to be rulers of thousands, and rulers of hundreds, rulers of fifties, and rulers of tens (Old Testament, Exodus, 18: 17–21).

If the Prophet Musa (*as*) felt hampered by his numerous responsibilities, and practiced delegation in previous times, contemporary Muslim leaders too should learn how to delegate.

When the leader delegates, he is saying, "Here is a task I wish you to perform. Here are the results I expect you to achieve within this period of time. I will assess your progress and what you accomplish in terms of your ability to accomplish these objectives." By delegating to a member, the leader assumes that the brother or sister is mature enough to assume responsibility for the task. The delegation process will not be effective unless a *specific* task is explicitly assigned to a member, some degree of authority is granted to the delegate, and the delegate is held accountable for completing his assignment.

To understand the process of delegation, two key terms need to be clarified: responsibility and accountability. **Responsibility** is the "obligation to undertake a specific duty or task within the organization. It can be assigned or assumed."[135] In this chapter, we are primarily concerned with responsibilities that are assigned. Examples of assigned responsibilities are completion of an annual report, mailing of membership renewal forms, and organization of a camp. When assigning a responsibility, a leader must ensure that he is asking his delegate to accomplish something realistic and within his control. A person who is not the treasurer of the organization cannot be held responsible for signing checks or balancing the accounts; he does not have the formal authority do so.

Accountability focuses on what a person has done with respect to a particular assignment. Did he or she perform the task? How well did he or she perform the task? Accountability provides the leader with feedback and enables him to intervene should the task be performed at an

---

[134] Al Habshi, Syed Othman (1987). "Development of Islamic Managerial and Administrative Practices: A Historical Perspective." *Seminar on Islamic Management.* Kuala Lumpur, Malaysia: Islamic Research and Training Institute.

[135] Steinmetz, pp. 10–11.

unacceptable level. A major reason why leaders may be reluctant to delegate, and prefer to handle everything themselves is that they do not hold their followers accountable for tasks that they have assigned to them. Accountability makes a delegate take ownership for the success and/or failure of the task, and motivates him or her to seek help before it is too late.

Let us consider the following case:[136]

> Assume that I am the leader of Dar-Es-Salaam Masjid in a large Eastern city of the USA. The *masjid* operates a bookstore, a full-time Islamic school, and several rental apartments. These apartments are rented out to students from local universities and community colleges. All renters must pay a deposit of one month's rent before an apartment is rented out to them. This deposit is returned to them when they leave provided the rental apartment is returned in reasonably clean and well-maintained condition.
>
> Riad is one of the members of the *masjid's* Board of Trustees. He is also the treasurer. I usually collect the monthly rental fee from the renters at the end of each month. These past two weeks, however, I was out of town, and Riad collected the rent during my absence. When I came back, he informed me of a problem that he had encountered. Anwar, one of our renters, was graduating and leaving for his home country. He wanted his rent deposit back immediately. Since I would not be back before Anwar had left, Riad inspected the apartment, and agreed on deductions from the deposit because of some carpet stains. The carpet would need to be professionally cleaned, but not replaced. Riad then returned the remainder of the deposit to Anwar.

Did Riad handle the situation correctly? Is this how a delegated task should be accomplished? The answer depends on a number of factors:

- What was the scope of Riad's job as treasurer of the *masjid?* How much autonomy did he have?

- How was the treasurer's job specified? Does the Constitution of the Board of Trustees include a list of what he can or cannot do, or were the specifics of his job implied through mutual understanding?

- What was the duration of Riad's rent collection task?

Since I had discussed how to handle such situations with Riad before, he handled the situation correctly. We had both agreed that he would collect the rent for me and perform any rent-related activity in my absence. In this case, he had performed what was required of him. Here is a different set of circumstances:

---

[136] Ibid., pp. 14–15. The hypothetical scenarios presented in this chapter were reworked from similar ones presented in Steinmetz (1976).

> Although treasurer of Dar-es-Salaam Masjid, Riad had never been involved in rent collection or any rent-related activity. When he had asked for guidance, I had indicated that I was rarely out of town, and that our student renters were always punctual with paying their rent. When Riad urged me to consider this possibility, I brushed his request aside, saying, "Don't worry so much. *Insha' Allah,* I will always be present to handle any rent-related problem. If I should ever be out of town, just rely on your gut feeling."

Is the above an example of effective delegation? Not really. It is more an illustration of vague leadership. I beat around the bush, and refused to provide any guidance or even to suggest some kind of procedure. I was lucky that Riad happened to deal with Anwar properly. Here is one last variation of the same scenario:

> I am performing Hajj, *al hamdu lillah* — my first after working so hard for many years. Before I left for Makkah, I convened the whole Board of Trustees of the mosque, and went over the tasks that would need to be performed during my absence. Riad was appointed as acting president, and was to perform all the activities that I usually do. He accepted his new responsibilities enthusiastically. During my absence, the *masjid* functioned flawlessly. After my return, I consulted with the Board of Trustees and the membership, and decided to create a new position, the Vice-President. Soon, *insha' Allah*, Riad will be moved into this position. In this manner, I can spend less time on rent collection, and more time on key outreach activities for the mosque.

In this last scenario, Riad had been given specific responsibilities and the commensurate responsibility to perform them. He is also being readied for greater responsibilities.

From the three above scenarios, delegation can be inferred to be the transfer of a portion of the leader's task to a follower or delegate. This transfer is temporary, and is usually not part of the role description of the delegate. A work assignment within the parameters of the delegate's job description is not a delegation. Unlike the usual leader-follower relationship where disobedience could be heavily punished, a follower may refuse a task that is being delegated to him without any fear of reprisal. However, any such refusal may deny him any chance of being trained for more challenging tasks.

Once a task is assigned properly to a delegate, and he accepts, there is a chance that this task may be subtly transformed into a permanent assignment, especially if the delegate performs extremely well initially. The danger of this change is that the nature of the relationship between the leader and the delegate will revert back to a boss-subordinate relationship once the delegated task is recast as a permanent work assignment. The delegate may feel locked out of immediate access to the leader, and may feel unmotivated since the delegated task is not what he himself agreed to perform, but something that is now being imposed on him.

Barriers to Delegation

Barriers to effective delegation may originate either from the leader delegating tasks or from the followers being delegated to or from both.

Why leaders are reluctant to delegate

The reluctance of leaders to delegate stems from both internal and external reasons. We will cover only two such reasons here in order that leaders and their followers can avoid them. An external reason leading to a lack of delegation is an organization's culture. A key internal reason is a leader's personality, specifically, a Type A personality (see Table 6-1 below).

Organization culture as an obstacle to delegation. Once an individual joins an organization, he or she will imbibe, or be socialized into, the culture that is specific to that organization. Culture can be defined as the shared norms, values, behavior patterns, rituals, and traditions in an organization.[137] In some organizations, delegation is frowned upon, and leaders of various committees are expected to be "in charge." Involving followers in key decisions and using a democratic style of leadership may violate organizational norms. In other organizations, delegation is a facade; the leader's wishes are being implemented through another party. One Islamic organization that we came across had a leader who ostensibly delegated, but in fact used the process to push his own decisions. After appointing various committee heads, he would intervene at each step, and steer their decisions from afar. By building an organization culture where committee heads were "rewarded" only if they implemented his decisions, he had developed a culture where the process of delegation had become totally distorted. In properly run organizations though, leaders are encouraged to mentor their second-in-command through delegation, and to involve them in major issues early on.

---

[137] Schein, E. H. (1997). *Organizational Culture and Leadership*. San Francisco, CA: Jossey-Bass, 2nd edition, p. 10.

Table 6-1:
Ten Reasons Given by Leaders for Being Reluctant to Delegate?

1. No one else is qualified to handle this responsibility except me.
2. I am a perfectionist; it must be done right.
3. I want the rewards, and do not want to share it with anybody else.
4. I do not want to look like I am getting soft.
5. I am uneasy asking my subordinates to do something for me especially when they look so busy.
6. By the time I finish explaining what needs to be done, I could have done it myself.
7. If I delegate too much, the organization may not need me anymore.
8. I do not like losing control.
9. When I delegate, I will still be responsible if something goes wrong.
10. Once I delegate, my superior will sidestep me if he needs any information about the delegated task. I will be out of the loop.

Type A Leaders. Type A leaders exhibit a great need for control. These leaders are very impatient with delays. They constantly measure how they are doing in comparison to others, and are competitive in almost every arena. They are aggressive in their social interaction, and get quite impatient with other coworkers. Finally, they work at multiple tasks simultaneously even when there is no deadline compelling them to do so. Type A individuals do not understand why others do not have the same sense of urgency about their work. They are poor delegators because they like to remain in control. As a result, they tend to prefer to work alone and do not do well in a team environment. Leaders who are Type A need to be matched to situations where such personality characteristics can be tolerated. A Type A person (whether as leader or follower) who is allowed to continue unchecked, may experience burnout. Hence, they need to be taught Islamic etiquette so that they can moderate their competitiveness and aggressiveness, and make full use of the *shura* process.

Why followers avoid being delegated to

Followers are not always eager to be delegated to. Some may feel that their autonomy is being taken away, and may react negatively. Others may simply not want the extra responsibility. There are several external and internal reasons why followers do not want the extra responsibility associated with a delegated task. Externally, the organization culture may dictate that all the rewards of a delegated activity be credited to the leader, and any blame for poor performance be attributed to the delegate.

As a result, followers may not enthusiastically embrace any delegated task. Internally, some followers may have an external locus of control, and feel that some nameless "they" are always manipulating them. As a result, they consistently refuse to be delegated to. The followers may also have found that if they delay long enough, the leader will step in and do the task himself. As a result, they play a waiting game. Other reasons why followers are reluctant to be delegated to are summarized in Table 6-2.

Table 6-2:
Ten Reasons Given by Followers to Avoid Being Delegated to

1.	I am not qualified to handle this responsibility.
2.	What is in it for me?
3.	If something goes wrong, I will get the criticism; if everything goes right, my superior will get all the rewards.
4.	I do not want to look like I am the leader's personal buddy.
5.	This work is below my superior skills.
6.	This work is not part of my job description. This task is the leader's responsibility.
7.	I do not like to receive criticism.
8.	What if this delegated task becomes permanently assigned to me?
9.	I do not like being imposed upon.
10.	If I delay long enough, the leader will step in and do it himself.

Delegation Guidelines

☑ **Select the delegate with the appropriate skill level, expertise and background.**

In delegating, it is very important to match the task or assignment to the skill level of the delegate. The Prophet (*saw*) and the subsequent Rightly Guided Caliphs (*ra*) were quite aware of the importance of matching the demands of an assignment to the level of development of a *sahāba*. One such example is 'Umar ibn al Khattab's (*ra*) choice of a commander of the task force to capture the city of al Ubullah. This city served as a massive arms depot for the Persian forces that were opposing the Muslims. With its internal fortresses and observation towers, it was considered impregnable. With almost every male in the city of Madinah involved in some campaign elsewhere, he had very few persons to choose from as a commander. He finally chose 'Utbah Ibn Ghazwan because of the following:

> ['Utbah] ... was a well-known *mujahid* who had fought at Badr, Uhud, al Khandaq and other battles. He had also fought at the terrible battle of Yamamah and emerged unscathed. He was, in fact, one of the first to accept Islam. He went on the first *hijrah* to Abyssinia but he had returned to stay with the Prophet in Makkah. He then went on *hijrah* to Madinah. This tall and imposing companion of the Prophet was known for his exceptional skill in the use of spears and arrows.[138]

Based on the above, we can see 'Umar chose 'Utbah because he was an experienced and courageous *mujahid*, a proven, skilled soldier, and a faithful companion of the Prophet (*saw*).

Leaders have to be careful in appointments for important positions because of the potential for good or mischief that such positions imply. This may be why the Prophet (*saw*) said, in a hadith transmitted by Al Hakim, "Whosoever delegates a position to someone when he sees that someone else is more competent (for the position), then surely he has cheated Allah, His Messenger, and all the Muslims."[139] Favoritism, nepotism, or any other bias in choosing a leader is thus ruled out.

✓ **Select a delegate with whom you have a reciprocal trusting relationship.**

In Islamic organizations, sometimes things do not work out. Under such circumstances, the relationship between a delegator and his or her delegate will be severely tested. The relationship is more likely to survive and endure if reciprocal trust and mutual respect exist between the two. As a result, they will not be suspicious of one another, and will help each other during hard times as much as they do during good times. Ali (*ra*), a companion of the Prophet Muhammad (*saw*), and the fourth Rightly Guided Caliph, understood the importance of appointing trustworthy persons as advisors. In his famous letter to Malik al Ashtar al Nakha'ī after the latter's appointment as Governor of Egypt, he stated the following:

> Gather honest, truthful, and pious people around you as your companions and friends. Train them not to flatter you, and not to seek your favor by false praises. Flattery and false praise create vanity and conceit; they make one lose sight of one's real self and duties.[140]

---

[138] Hamid, AbdulWahid. (1995). *Companions of the Prophet*. Leicester: MELS, vol. 1., pp. 180–1.

[139] Ibn Taymiyyah. *Al Siyasatus Shariah Fi Islaahir Raa'ie war Rai'iyyah*. Translated by K.H. Firdaus (1977), p. 42, and cited by Al Habshi.

[140] Behzadnia and Denny.

☑ Delegate both the pleasant and the unpleasant, the easy and the challenging.

If only the unpleasant and most difficult tasks are delegated by the leader, then this is a case of "dumping."[141] For the leader to delegate effectively, he should allot a variety of tasks. The Prophet (*saw*) was clearly aware of this. During the battle of Khandaq, he joined the Muslim army in digging the ditch. At Uhud, he was in the forefront and personally fought off the challenge from Ubayy bin Khalaf. During the conquest of the fortress of Khaybar, Ali (*ra*) himself (made commander of the Muslim forces by the Prophet) carried the gate on which the Muslims ascended and were able to conquer the fortress.[142]

☑ Delegate ahead.

Sometimes, leaders forget that their delegates have their own personal responsibilities. By delegating ahead, leaders ensure that delegates will have enough time to ask for additional information if they should need it. The delegates will be able to experiment before trying a final solution, and to learn from their initial attempts at performing the task. Hence, delegates will not be inconvenienced, and will be able to fit the task within their schedule. Last minute delegation is poor planning on the part a leader, and may place undue pressure on the delegate.

☑ Delegate in chunks.

Leaders should not delegate too complex a task or only minor pieces of the same task. If the task is too complex, the delegate may lack the skills to manage all of it, and may experience cognitive overload. However, if the task is too minute and simplistic, he or she may get bored. Unless the delegate can clearly identify with a whole task, he or she may not be as motivated. Gluing 20,000 stamps onto envelopes is not as motivating as being in charge of a whole mailing process for a national convention, which involves a series of steps that range from obtaining a mailing address list to stuffing and mailing envelopes. The whole mailing process is a complete task and provides a real feeling of challenge to a qualified delegate. Please be aware that some delegates may have a low n_{ach} (need for achievement), and may prefer to be assigned relatively simple tasks that others would consider boring. The n_{ach} can be defined as a desire to do well in demanding situations. Research indicates that people with a high n_{ach} tend to assume responsibility for solving problems, set moderately challenging goals for themselves, and to value feedback

---

[141] Nahavandi, A. (1997). *The Art and Science of Leadership*. Upper Saddle River, NJ: Prentice-Hall, 1997, p. 163.

[142] As-Suyuti, Jalal al-Din (1996). *The History of the Khalifahs Who Took the Right Way*. London: Ta-Ha Publishers, p. 175.

about their performance. Match the level of complexity or difficulty of
the task to the level of n_{ach} of your delegate.[143]

☑ Delegate precisely.

Unless each delegate knows specifically what is expected of him or her
and by when, chaos is likely to result. Inaccurate delegation also makes
it difficult to establish some type of control system to verify that
delegated tasks are on track, and that expected outputs and outcomes are
being produced. Controls do not have to be overly sophisticated or
intrusive: mere visual observation accompanied by a regularly scheduled
briefing session are often quite adequate. In larger, more complex
organizations, elaborate performance evaluation systems may be set into
place.

☑ Delegate, don't abdicate.

One of the most severe mistakes that a leader can make is to abandon
the delegate after assigning a task. Sometimes this abandonment takes
place because the leader is not comfortable with the task that he or she
has delegated. He may still have access to resources and contacts that
the delegate will need if the delegated task is to be performed. Instead of
deserting the delegate, the leader can still provide a supportive
environment and thereby maximize the chances of success.

☑ Give credit.[144]

Take a few minutes to read the following two scenarios. Here is
scenario 1:

> This morning I went to the office after coming back from the largest Muslim
> convention in the North American continent. I had been in charge of
> managing the whole convention, and expected my president to be quite
> happy with the manner in which the convention went. However, he burst
> into my office and started quizzing me about the hotel arrangements during
> the convention. He was especially upset that one of his mentors had not
> been lodged in a guest suite at the convention hotel. I was so taken aback
> by his comments that I did not mention the many areas of the convention
> that had worked without a problem.

Here is scenario 2:

> This morning, I went to the office after coming back from the largest Muslim
> convention in the North American continent. I had been in charge of
> managing the whole convention, and expected my president to be quite
> happy with the manner in which the convention went. After he came into my
> office, he told me that I had done an excellent job, and that he wanted me to
> present a special report on the convention to the Board. I mentioned that

---

[143] McClelland, D. (1961) *The Achieving Society.* Princeton, NJ: Van Nostrand.
[144] Engel, Herbert. M. (1990) *How to Delegate: A Guide to Getting Things Done.*
Houston, TX.

one of his mentors had not been lodged in a guest suite at the convention hotel, but he said that was a minor detail, and he would take care of the situation. I was so relieved and pleased that I volunteered for any other similar assignment in the future. He told me that he would keep me in mind.

In Scenario 1, the delegate is being reprimanded twice: he is not rewarded for managing a massive convention and he is criticized for what he perceives to be a minor detail within the whole convention setup. The leader is more concerned about his personal relationship with his mentor than about the success of a major activity of his organization.

In Scenario 2, the leader or delegator keeps things in perspective. He positively rewards the excellent performance of his delegate, and offers to solve the minor problem with his mentor. More importantly, he obtains the delegate's future support by letting him make a report to the Board. The delegate is energized and ready to accept another similar assignment. In both cases, the delegator is responding to the performance of the delegate. In Scenario 1, the response is clearly inappropriate; in scenario 2, the delegator is building the delegate's self-confidence and is rewarding him appropriately. Again, Ali (*ra*) in his letter to Malik al Ashtar recommends the following:

Everyone should receive the treatment his deeds make him deserve.[145]

Table 6-3 provides a checklist to guide you during the delegation process.

Though one of the most important ingredients of effective delegation is assigning a specific task to a member, the leader must remember that delegation is difficult. It is affected both by the leader's leadership style as well as by the culture of the organization. Leaders with a *directive* or autocratic style of leadership find it relatively difficult to share their power with anybody else. They forget one of the golden principles of delegation: the more power you give away, the more power you have.[146] Instead, the leader is reluctant to delegate because he thinks that he can do a better job himself, or that it will take too long to explain to his members what needs to be done. Even when he delegates, a directive leader will be tempted to *overcontrol* his follower by frequent visits, phone calls, or requests for reports. Alternately, a leader with a *supportive* style may demonstrate a lack of interest toward his delegate, and thus *undercontrol*. The leader needs to strike a balance between overcontrol and undercontrol, depending upon the maturity level of his delegate. Finally, some leaders do not delegate because they feel that other brothers or sisters are too busy. As a result, they bear the whole

---

[145] Ali (*ra*). *To the Commander in Chief from Imam Ali to Malik al Ashtar*. Translation by Behzadnia, A and Denny. S.
[146] Kouzes and Posner (1995).

burden of running the organization on their shoulders, and end up overworked and stressed. Unfortunately, the organization, too, may collapse after this leader departs because he has failed to train others in leadership skills.

Table 6-3: Delegation Checklist

Select the appropriate brother/sister.	Do not assign a task that is beyond the current knowledge or skill level of your member.
Select a delegate with whom you have a reciprocal trusting relationship.	Neither the leader nor the delegate should be second guessing each other or attempting to keep the other party "off-balance."
Delegate both the pleasant and the unpleasant, the easy and the challenging.	Do not assign only unpleasant tasks, otherwise, motivation and commitment will suffer.
Delegate ahead.	Do not wait until the last minute to delegate.
Delegate in chunks.	Delegating a complex task may overwhelm a delegate. Break it up into manageable chunks. An initial small success with a chunk of the task may act as a motivator.
Delegate precisely.	Delegate to someone specifically; delegate a specific task; delegate within a specific time frame.
Delegate; don't abdicate.	Be willing to provide your follower with the necessary authority to fulfil his responsibility. You will, however, be ultimately responsible for the outcome.
Give credit.	Behavior that is rewarded will be repeated; behavior that is not rewarded will not be repeated.

Improved communication between leader and members can overcome many of the barriers to effective delegation. To the extent that the leader, as coach, understands the strengths and weaknesses of his or her followers, he or she can match the tasks he or she wishes to delegate with the appropriate brother or sister. Followers who are clear about their assignments and feel that their leaders are supportive and trust their abilities will be more willing to be delegated to. For this type of relationship to occur, leaders and delegates must share each other's thoughts and concerns as candidly as possible. In this regard, the letter that Ali (ra) wrote to Malik al Ashtar, his Governor of Egypt, stands out in history as one of the most important documents on leadership.[147] It is especially important from a delegation perspective. In this letter, the Caliph specifies exactly what is expected of an administrator/leader. The following is an excerpt of special relevance to this chapter. Ali (*ra*) is stressing the importance of good Islamic character and behavior to Malik:

> Beware not to develop the trait of self-admiration and self-appreciation. Do not get vain about the good points that you find in your character or the good deeds that you have done. Do not let flattery and compliments make you conceited and egotistical ...

> Do not boast of the favors and kindnesses that you have done for your subjects; do not try to make them realize this. Do not think too much of the good you have done for them. Do not go back over the promises made. All of these habits are very ugly features of one's character. The practice of boasting over the favors done undoes the good done. The habit of exaggerating and thinking very highly of your good actions will make you lose the guidance of Allah. The custom of breaking one's promises is highly disliked both by Allah and by man. The Merciful, Allah, says, "It highly displeases Allah that you do not fulfill your promises."

> Do not be hasty and precipitous in your decisions and actions; however, when the time comes to make a decision or to act, do not be lazy; do not waste time, and do not show weakness. When you do not find a true way to do the thing on hand, do not continue the wrong way. And when you find the correct solution, do not be lethargic in adopting it. In short, do everything in its proper time and in its proper way, and keep everything in its proper place.

> Do not reserve for yourself anything which is common property to all and in which others have equal rights. Do not close your eyes to the glaring malpractices of the officers, miscarriages of justice, and misuse of rights. You will be held responsible for the wrong thus done to others ... Be careful to control your temper, your anger, your desire to be arrogant and vain. Take care of your hands when you are delivering punishment. And watch the sharpness of your tongue when you are saying harsh things. The best way to achieve this is not to be hasty in remarks and to delay delivering punishment so that your temper may be abated and you get complete control over yourself. This cannot be achieved unless you constantly remember that your return is to Allah, and unless [your] fear [of Him] overcomes every other sentiment.

> You must always try to remember the good and useful things done in the past, the activities of a just and benign government, the good deeds done by it, the good laws promulgated, the orders and traditions of the Holy Prophet (*saw*), the orders of Allah given out in His Holy [Qur'an], and the things that

---

[147] Al Buraey, pp. 266–7.

you have seen me do or have heard me say. Follow the good actions and advice found therein...[148]

How Effective Are You at Delegating?

Consider carefully the following ten statements,[149] which characterize many of the delegating issues that you will face. For each statement, circle "A" if you *agree* and "D" if you *disagree*. The "delegate" is the brother or sister to whom you have given an assignment. After you are done, check your answers on the next page.

1. It's a good idea to check up on your delegate when he or she least expects it.	A D
2. Doubting the abilities of a person as a delegate until that person proves himself or herself is a good practice.	A D
3. When communicating with your delegate, there's nothing wrong with treating him as you might treat your own children.	A D
4. Your delegate asks for help on some problem. Probably the first thing you should determine is whether he or she's trying to unload the delegation back to you.	A D
5. Effective time management may result in fewer delegations.	A D
6. Delegates who deliberately fail to inform their delegators about the results of a delegation are probably not to be trusted.	A D
7. Your delegate is experiencing a problem, and asks for advice. Tell the delegate that if he or she can't figure it out, you'll choose someone else next time.	A D
8. Complex delegations, divided among several delegates, must be tightly controlled by the leader.	A D
9. There are some responsibilities that a leader should not delegate.	A D
10. It is a good idea to delegate the same function to two persons in order to observe who will do the better job.	A D

---

[148] Behzadnia and Denny, p. 24.
[149] Adapted from Engel, H., pp. 1–5.

Answers to the Delegation Questionnaire[150]

1. *Disagree*. Islam is typically against sneaking up on someone. Indeed, Allah admonishes us against this type of behavior:

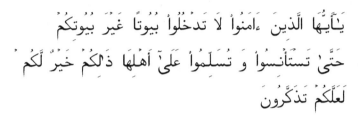

> O you who believe! enter not houses other than your own until you have asked permission and saluted those in them: that is best for you in order that you may heed (what is seemly). (Nur, 24:27)

2. *Disagree*. Know your delegate's capabilities and skills *before* you assign a responsibility to him. Doubting someone after you delegate to that person is likely to result in a self-fulfilling prophesy, and doom him or her to failure.
3. *Disagree*. Normally, you are not the delegate's parent, and he or she is not your son or daughter. Treat the delegate as an *adult* even if you are related.
4. *Disagree*. Determine first why he or she is asking you for help. Listen actively. Make certain that the delegate really needs help before offering to help. His reply will let you determine whether he is trying to manoeuver you into doing his work.
5. *Disagree*. Effective time management should encourage delegations throughout the whole organization.
6. *Agree*. The key words are "deliberately fail to inform …" Delegates must provide an accurate report of the results, whether good or bad. Since the delegator may base himself or herself on this report for future decisions, misinforming him or her may lead to worse problems. Should delegates in fact deliberately hold back information about the results, they should probably not be trusted.
7. *Disagree*. Before warning the delegate about the next delegation, listen to him or her. The delegate may need advice. Advice and doing the work for the person are not the same thing.

---

[150] Ibid., pp. 242–8. We have modified some of the answers to fit an Islamic context.

8. *Depends.* Typically, there is no reason why complex delegations cannot be segmented among several delegates. However, should this be an emergency, centralization may be needed, and some measure of tight control may be required to avoid fatal errors.

9. *Agree.* Delegation does not mean abdication. Many responsibilities cannot, and should not be delegated, such as strategic planning, evaluation of personnel that report directly to you, and major policy issues.

10. *Disagree.* There is a good possibility that the two delegates may find out what you have done, and feel that you do not trust either of them.

Chapter 7
Using Multiple Frames in Leadership

Besides coaching others, a leader needs to engage in self-development. One of the most important skills that he must learn is the ability to look at a situation from multiple perspectives or frames. The core of using multiple frames or *reframing* is in examining one situation through different lenses in order to obtain a more complete understanding of the facts.[151] An effective leader adjusts or changes his frame when what he perceives does not make sense. This skill will allow him to be more incisive and more flexible in devising new approaches to a situation. Practice this skill; it will help you be less myopic and self-centered, *insha' Allah.* To illustrate how reframing works, we will work through the case of Bassaam Abu Dawud.[152]

Bassaam Abu Dawud

Imagine that you are Bassaam Abu Dawud, headed to your company's headquarters. You have been working for this corporation, Newtech, since you graduated from the university, and have steadily worked your way up to the position of regional manager. Recently, you have been promoted to replace Said Khalidi as Chief Executive Officer. The Board of Directors believes that Khalidi is the source of many of the problems that Newtech is facing with respect to its products and services. The company is losing market share, and its product and service offerings are not keeping up with changing customer needs. Khalidi has also stopped

---

[151] Bolman, Lee G. & Deal, Terrence E. (1997). *Reframing Organizations: Artistry, Choice and Leadership.* San Francisco, CA: Jossey Bass.

[152] The contents of this scenario are similar to one developed by Bolman and Deal (1997). It has been reworked to fit the context of a Muslim organization, but the characters in the scenario are all fictitious and any resemblance to any actual person or events is purely coincidental.

paying attention to any direction or advice from the Board of Directors. Said, however, was one of the first employees at Newtech. Hired a decade ago, he has long considered himself to be a "founding member" of the company. Many of the people whom you will be in charge of have known him for years, and are still loyal to him. He is difficult to get along with, and quite dogmatic. He is being moved to another part of Newtech, but has been asked to train you for the next 10 days.

This morning, you are meeting with the Executive Task Force, a committee of the top managers who will be working with you to turn Newtech around. Khalidi has been requested to make a presentation on the current status of the company. When you enter your office suite, Mariam Nabeela, your executive assistant, greets you rather abruptly. Thinking nothing of it, you walk over to the Conference Room where the meeting is to take place. Said Khalidi is sitting at the head of the table, talking to your new staff. Instead of replying to your greeting, he says, "I am busy explaining to these people how to handle things after I leave. I do not like being interrupted when I am in conference. Ask Mariam to let you know when you can meet with me."

Put yourself in the role of Bassaam Abu Dawud. Here are four possible scenarios for how you might deal with Said's behavior:

Scenario 1:

Said: I am busy explaining to these people how to handle things after I leave. I do not like being interrupted when I am in conference. Ask Mariam to let you know when you can meet with me.

Bassaam: I have been appointed to replace you from this morning on. This meeting should rightly be chaired by me.

Said: Just a minute, here! The President himself asked me to help you. I am only doing what was requested of me, but if you feel you do not need my help, I can leave now.

Bassaam: You can leave after you have trained me. From this moment on, I am taking over this meeting. Do you wish to start your presentation now?

Said: I find your behavior unacceptable. If you are going to push your way around, I will stop everything that I am doing, and leave. After all, Mr. Bassaam is the boss now, isn't he, guys?

In scenario 1, Bassaam is relying primarily on his new position's authority. He is forcing Said to yield. However, Bassaam's use of his position power may humiliate Said in front of his loyal subordinates, and create future problems with them. Bassaam could have handled the conversation in the following manner:

Alternate scenario 1:

Said: I am busy explaining to these people how to handle things after I leave. I do not like being interrupted when I am in conference. Ask Mariam to let you know when you can meet with me.

Bassaam: This is my first meeting, and I have so much to learn. Said, can you advise me on some of the key issues that I need to start working on? I can really benefit from your experience.

Said: All right! I will try to help you out. I have been in this business for decades. Can you give me a couple of minutes to get some minor details out of the way?

Bassaam: I am very detail oriented. I believe that if you take care of the trees, the forest will take of itself. What kind of details are you discussing?

Said: Office stuff, and secretarial help.

Bassaam: Please, go right ahead. I will just sit back here and listen. I have a lot to learn from all of you, and after Mr. Said is done with his presentation later, I would very much like to brainstorm on what we can do as a team to help Newtech. Specifically, I am sure that each of you has ideas about how we can make this place take off. I would like to hear from each of you later. Now, Said, please continue your meeting.

In the alternate scenario, Bassaam does not push his weight around. He is firm and focused, but manages to use Said's own arguments to enlist him. Finally, he does not capitulate in front of Said. He is in control, and sets the agenda for the remainder of the meeting.

Here is a second scenario of how Bassaam could have dealt with the situation we outlined earlier.

Scenario 2:

Said: I am busy explaining to these people how to handle things after I leave. I do not like being interrupted when I am in conference. Ask Mariam to let you know when you can meet with me.

Bassaam: I am sorry I interrupted you. I did not mean to barge in. Do you mind if I pour myself some tea, and just watch?

Said: Yes, I do mind. Don't you trust me to handle a meeting by myself? I am a big boy, you know. Mariam will let you know when I am about to make the presentation.

Bassaam: Thank you for your understanding. I did not mean to put you down in any way. I will wait in the hallway until you are ready.

In scenario 2, Bassaam is being too appeasing. After all, the meeting is supposed to be one that he is in charge of, and where Said comes to make a presentation. Although Bassaam has avoided a confrontation, Said has backed him down, and he is likely to be seen as weak by his future managers.

Alternate scenario 2:

Said: I am busy explaining to these people how to handle things after I leave. I do not like being interrupted when I am in conference. Ask Mariam to let you know when you can meet with me.

Bassaam: I am sorry I interrupted you. I did not mean to impose myself. Since I am already here, let me introduce myself to everyone here. (*He walks around the table, greets everyone cheerfully, and then addresses Said again.*) I want very much to get to know everybody, and to help in whatever way I can. Please proceed.

Said: I will. If you have any pointers, please save them for the end.

Bassaam: No problem, Said. I believe that I am one who is here to learn from you all. Please carry on. When you are done with your presentation, can we have lunch together and talk about this transition period?

In alternate scenario 2, Bassaam subtly made allies of the other participants and did not allow himself to be kicked out of the room. He listened actively. By recognizing that he too can learn from Said, he has turned the latter into a teacher/mentor rather than an adversary. His request to be a silent observer/student is difficult to turn down.

Scenario 3:

Said: I am busy explaining to these people how to handle things after I leave. I do not like being interrupted when I am in conference. Ask Mariam to let you know when you can meet with me.

Bassaam: I am the new boss, and can come and go as it suits me. You are supposed to help me, not the other way around.

Said: You may be replacing me, but don't be in such a hurry to throw me out on the street. I have a lot more experience than you. After all, I am one of the founding members of Newtech.

Bassaam: You are also responsible for its current problems. Look, stay if you wish. Otherwise, please leave. I do not have time to waste. I will be sure to report your degree of cooperation to the Board.

Bassaam is being very aggressive here, and will probably win this skirmish; however, he is quite close to being arrogant, and may be branded as such by the others present. This is a label that sticks in the long term and may hamper his effectiveness.

Alternate scenario 3:

Said: I am busy explaining to these people how to handle things after I leave. I do not like being interrupted when I am in conference. Ask Mariam to let you know when you can meet with me.

Bassaam: Said, let us be candid. I need you and you need me. Do you object to working with me?

Said: Look here! I am the one trying to hand you the place on a platter. What more do you want?

Bassaam: Don't misunderstand me. I want to turn this place around as quickly as possible, and I would hope that you, too, want the same. Do you?

Said: Of course, I want the place to succeed. Why else would we be meeting?

Bassaam: Great, then. Let us get to work then. I know we will make a great team, and I will be sure to mention that everybody is helping out when I make my report to the Board later this week.

Bassaam here delicately steps over any obstacles that Said places in his path. He is firm, but not gratuitously confrontational. He uses the "you scratch my back, I scratch your back" approach to bind everybody together in a common effort to help out the company. At the end, he implicitly uses his reward and position power to promise everybody a reward: a good word from him to the Board. In this alternate scenario, everybody has won something, and no one was trampled upon.

Scenario 4:

Said: I am busy explaining to these people how to handle things after I leave. I do not like being interrupted when I am in conference. Ask Mariam to let you know when you can meet with me.

Bassaam: Said, I am here to help. Can't we behave as Muslims and start with the right *niyat*?

Said: We are already behaving Islamically. In fact, as a founding member of this corporation, I am only trying to benefit you with my experience.

Bassaam: Look, you are only helping fix problems that occurred under *your* watch! Your position was an *amānah*, and what did you accomplish with it?

Said: My *niyat* is clear: I tried my best, and Allah only can be my judge in this regard.

Bassaam: Again, my task is to fix previous mistakes and turn the company around. As *amir*,[153] I need your cooperation — all of you. If you feel you cannot cooperate with me, please let me know right now. (*Everybody remains silent, staring at the conference table or at the*

---

[153] *Amir* means leader.

walls). *Al hamdu lillah!* I knew I could count on all of you. Now let us get to work.

Bassaam is relying on an Islamic approach. However, he is not using it appropriately. The manner in which he accuses Said of having betrayed his *amānah* is potentially hurtful. He should not have to emphasize his "role" as leader since that is likely to turn the people in the room against him. He has been appointed as leader; he has not yet proven to this group of people that he has earned the right to be their leader.

Alternate scenario 4:

Said: I am busy explaining to these people how to handle things after I leave. I do not like being interrupted when I am in conference. Ask Mariam to let you know when you can meet with me.

Bassaam: Said, you *are* dedicated! I am pleased that you are all already working. May Allah be pleased with your efforts! I believe if we all work together like this and set up clear priorities, we will, *insha' Allah,* succeed.

Said: Of course, but I do not have much time right now. Can you give us a couple of minutes for some unfinished business?

Bassaam: Please include me in your discussion then. I want to turn this place around as quickly as possible, and I want a running start. I would hope that all of us here want the company to survive and prosper. Isn't that what you want?

Said: Of course.

Bassaam: Great, then. Thank you for agreeing to guide us during this critical transition. Let us roll up our sleeves. Before we agree on an agenda, may I suggest that we recite a short *du'a* ? Said, can you please do that for us? (*Said raises up his hands and leads in a short dua*) Now if you do not mind, I will sit back here and be a silent observer. I just wish to learn from you as you wrap up any unfinished business.

Bassaam here is again using an Islamic approach, but he is doing so correctly. At no point does he humiliate Said. Rather, he is firm, but humble. By focusing on core Islamic values such as respect for others and by appealing to Allah for help and guidance before starting anything, he has inspired everybody to be in the right frame of mind. *Insha' Allah,* they should all be willing to work together as a team.

The Four Frames

In scenario 1 and its alternate, Bassaam is using the *structural frame*. The organization is seen as a machine. Structures are designed to be situationally appropriate, i.e., to fit an organization's strategy (mission and goals), environment, and technology. Organization participants are given specific responsibilities in accordance with the role they are assigned while rules, procedures, and a chain of command are used to coordinate activities. Task orientation is critical, and Bassaam encourages his managers to think in terms of priorities and actions to deal with these.

In scenario 2 and its alternate, Bassaam uses the *human resource frame*: The organization is seen as an extended family, populated by individuals that have needs, feelings, skills, and limitations. Organizational participants can engage in learning. The issue is how to fit the organization to the people so that they can accomplish what they are supposed to while feeling rewarded in what they do.

In scenario 3 and its alternate, Bassaam uses the *political frame*. The organization is seen as an arena. Organization participants have interests that are sometimes conflicting, and compete for scarce resources. As a result, they form coalitions around specific issues, and engage in bargaining and negotiation. Power and politics are frequently used to solve problems and conflicts.

In scenario 4 and its alternate, Bassaam used the *Islamic frame*. The Islamic frame is integrative. It involves components of all three of the above frames, but its assumptions are different. Although conflict is viewed as natural with both positive and negative consequences, the leader must attempt to manage it with the appropriate *niyat*.

Table 7-1 describes in detail several key organizational processes relating to the Islamic frame. These processes have been described in earlier chapters either implicitly or explicitly, and are summarized below:

Strategic planning. The first three tasks of strategic planning are: performing a SWOT analysis (to be discussed in the next chapter), developing a vision statement, and enunciating the mission of the organization. The organization is seen as a *jamā 'at*. Strategic planning, taking care of personnel needs and working with their skills and limitations, as well using power in the manner discussed earlier in this book are all part of the Islamic frame.

Decision-making. Islam's emphasis on *shura* or a divinely enjoined consultative process of decision making has been discussed. The Islamic leader is not a self-centered, egotistical decision-maker.

Leading. We have covered at length the foundational bases of Islamic leadership as well as its primary focus on spreading the Message of Allah. We have demonstrated how Islamic leadership is intrinsically ethical. The primary function of a Muslim leader is toward the good, and a leader must behave with and emphasize integrity. Islam, as a *dīn* or complete way of life, becomes the all-encompassing thread through all of his or her actions. The *niyat* of the leader is always important. Problems take place when Islamic values and rituals are devalued and when the *niyat* of the persons involved is ambiguous or self-serving.

Evaluating. Through the discussion on reward and coercive power as well as on the evaluation component of coaching, we have shown how rewards or punishments are used in Islam to nurture Muslim followers. When warranted by circumstances, the leader is to give his or her followers the benefit of the doubt and to err on the side of leniency.

Communication. Integrity and truth are the core of any communication between a leader and his or her followers.

Table 7-1: Organizational Processes according to the Islamic Frame

Process	Islamic Frame
Strategic Planning	Use strategies to coordinate; gatherings and other rituals to involve everybody and build symbolic and substantive commitment.
Decision Making	*Shura* is divinely decreed, and is binding after a rational and open consultative process. A rational approach to decision-making is encouraged, but does not replace divine guidance and inspiration.
Leading	Emphasizes the good, and maintains image of trust, integrity and responsiveness; unites rather than divides.
Evaluating	Rewards, punishes or helps in order to facilitate growth (spiritual and otherwise) of follower.
Communication	Transmit facts, exchange information and inspire via positive, gentle words. Seeking and telling the truth is of the utmost priority.
Goal setting	Goals focus on serving Allah, and incorporate shared values within Islamic framework.
Motivation	Internal and external incentives, but always driven by the desire to please Allah. Rewards in the Hereafter are far superior to any reward to be earned in this life.

Goal setting. No goal is worthy except what advances Islam and the cause of Allah.

Motivation. The only incentive that drives Muslim leaders and followers is the pleasure of Allah. Any reward in this *dunya* is by definition finite and limited, and pales in comparison to the rewards in the *akhira*. Both the leader and the followers are to be motivated by intrinsic (including spiritual) and extrinsic incentives, but the extrinsic incentives in this life cannot supplant the desire to work towards better and eternal rewards in the life hereafter.

Chapter 8
A Model of Leadership Effectiveness

One of the best models of effective leadership has been proposed by Kouzes and Posner.[154] This model consists of five basic steps with two phases per step. Table 8-1 summarizes the Kouzes and Posner model.

Table 8-1: A Model of Leadership Effectiveness

Steps	Phases
Challenge the process	a. Search for opportunities b. Experiment and take risks
Inspire a shared vision	a. Envision the future b. Enlist others
Enable others to act	a. Foster collaboration b. Strengthen others
Model the way	a. Set the example b. Plan small wins
Encourage the heart	a. Recognize individual contributions b. Celebrate accomplishments

Step 1. Challenging the Process

Leadership is an active, not a passive process. During the early days of the *Ikhwan al Muslimin,* Hassan al Banna did not wait for people to join

---

[154] Kouzes, J. M. and Posner, B. Z. (1995). *The Leadership Challenge.* San Francisco, CA: Jossey-Bass.

the movement; he went out and actively sought them. While ineffectual leaders sit around, waiting for Allah to help, successful Muslim leaders challenge the status quo, articulate an impelling vision and mission, and then ask Allah for help. In challenging the process, leaders have to be innovative. They often need to redefine the process in a way that tears down the physical and mental barriers imposed by others on the Muslim community. For example, dynamic Muslim leadership in India is refusing to allow Muslims to be labelled and classified as "untouchables." Similarly, in the United States the US Postal Service is considering issuing a stamp commemorating Islam. This idea sprang to life when a Muslim child from elementary school suggested the idea to his mother, and the suggestion was eventually championed by the International Union of Muslim Women. Recently, an American college professor publicly defamed Muslims in one of his classes. After the Council on American Islamic Relations (CAIR) intervened and demanded that the college impose disciplinary procedures, the educational institution did. This professor is no longer working there anymore.

In challenging the process, leaders search for opportunities both internally and externally. They look for ways to change or improve the status quo. These opportunities may include an innovative new service or activity, a reorganization, or a realignment of the mission of the organization. To help them in their search process, leaders need to use *shura* and consult with people both inside and outside the organization. Members use many of the services the organization provides, and can provide critical insights since they are closest to problem areas or to external constituents.

Leaders also experiment and take risks while challenging the process. They do so with the understanding that their efforts may not always succeed. Each failure, however, can be viewed as a learning opportunity. For example, let us assume that you are learning how to play soccer. If you stand behind the ball, but do not try to kick the ball, what have you learned? How can you improve your soccer skills without making an initial effort?

Step 2. Inspiring a Shared Vision

In challenging the status quo, a leader needs to have a vision of what the organization needs to accomplish. This is his or her main task. A vision is critical because it is the source of the mission statement and long-term strategy of the organization. The vision of the leader does not need to be detailed. In developing a vision, the leader needs to answer the following question: What is our organization seeking to do and to become? For example, the vision of the leader of an Islamic community association may be to help Muslims in the community act as one body.

A vision can be extremely motivating. Muslims need to believe in the future envisioned for this Ummah by the Prophet (*saw*). Their leaders must keep them focused on this vision, whether in triumph or in defeat, in times of munificence or in times of scarcity. Wherever they are, in whatever condition they may be, Muslim leaders must keep the Ummah moving toward this vision. Unfortunately, as depicted in Table 8-2, the process of visioning can suffer from several defects.

Table 8-2: Where Does Defective Vision Come From?

	Sources of Defective Vision[155]
Egocentricism	The vision reflects a preoccupation with the personal needs of the leader rather than the needs of the Ummah or of the local community.
Resource Gap	The leader has miscalculated the resources needed to implement the vision.
Closed System Perspective	The leader has misunderstood or underestimated the impact of external environmental forces on the vision, and hence, the vision is rigid and not adaptable.
Group Think	The leader may use *shura* to consult others in defining the vision, but all members think alike, and suffer from similar tunnel vision.

Egocentricism. The vision of the amir should not be self-centered or limited to the interests of special factions, groups, or nationalities. Islam is against the concept of *asabiyyah,* where people put the needs of their group or clan ahead of the needs of the whole community. To avoid this defect, the leader needs to involve as many members as possible with the appropriate expertise in the development of the organization's vision. By so doing, he will, *insha' Allah,* ensure their commitment to the vision. *Shura* must be an integral part of this process. The key idea is that the vision of the leader needs to be shared by brothers and sisters under his direction in order to increase their commitment to its implementation.

---

[155] Adapted from J. A. Conger. (1990). The dark side of leadership, *Organizational Dynamics.* New York: American Management Association. Autumn, p. 45.

Resource gap. Often, the leader may underestimate the resources it will take to achieve the vision. To avoid this mistake, the leader may engage in an analysis of the internal strengths and weaknesses of the organization as well as the external opportunities and threats faced by the organization. This analysis is called a SWOT (Strengths, Weaknesses, Opportunities, and Threats). An example of a SWOT of a hypothetical Muslim organization is depicted in Table 8-3.

Table 8-3: Example of a SWOT Analysis

Internal Strengths	Internal Weaknesses
1. Our members possess a variety of skills, and are dedicated.	1. The size of our organization's membership is small in comparison to the size of the Muslim Community.
2. Our organization has earned a national reputation.	2. Our organization depends on monthly donations and lacks a dedicated source of funds.
3. Our organization owns its head office and a full-time Islamic school.	3. There is continuous strife among various factions in our community based on their country of origin.
4. The organization puts out a monthly newsletter.	4. There is a lack of continuity in leadership since the same people keep volunteering for work.
External Opportunities	**External Threats**
1. The Muslim community is growing.	1. A new organization has emerged and is providing services identical to ours.
2. The internet provides us with the opportunity to do *da'wah* both within and outside our community.	2. The media coverage of Muslims is harsh and negative.
3. The number of non-Muslims interested in Islam is increasing.	3. National political leaders are increasingly more hostile toward Muslims.
4. The organization has not yet tapped into the funds allocated by the government to minorities.	4. Legislation restricting fundraising for and transmittal of funds to Muslim causes has been recently passed.

The above SWOT analysis enables the leader to assess the resource gap between the resources controlled by the organization and the resources it needs to tap into key external opportunities or to counter external threats.

By carrying out a SWOT analysis in conjunction with the process of visioning, the leader and key members of the community will develop a vision that is realistic. The vision should provide stretch, but should not be one that is impossible even in the long term. For example, a vision such as "To become the leading religious media outlet in North America" is an impressive vision for a new Muslim media organization; however, such a vision may take an extremely long time to happen, and may discourage organizational members in the short term. Instead, a vision that would state "To become one of the leading Islamic media outlets in New York City" may be more manageable and achievable within a decade. Leaders must have vision, but they must also be realistic.

Closed system perspective. A leader who maps out a path for his organization without taking into account what is happening on the outside is acting as though his organization is a closed system. Several Muslim organizations have fallen into this trap. Initially effective, the organization becomes somewhat disconnected with external events as it increases in size. Eventually, its services no longer address the changing needs of the Muslim and non-Muslim communities. The SWOT analysis technique illustrated in Table 8-3 can help an organization scan its external environment for emerging opportunities and threats, and plan accordingly. Leaders of Islamic organizations should set time aside for a *yearly* SWOT analysis. During this analysis, they need to scrutinize both their internal and external environments, revisit their strategic plan and adjust their vision statement if need be.

Groupthink. The process of *shura* may be distorted. If the leader surrounds himself by unquestioning members, the outcome of the consultative process will be limited to validating his decisions. The drive for consensus and simultaneous suppression of dissent is known as *groupthink.* Leaders must be aware of this dysfunctional aspect of group decision-making; they must ensure that members who are consulted are not afraid of voicing their opinion, even if it contradicts everybody else's. This principle is what Ali *(ra)* was stressing when he wrote to Malik al Ashtar:

> Gather honest, truthful, and pious people around you as your companions and friends. Train them not to flatter you, and not to seek your favor by false praises. ... Try to realize that a ruler can create goodwill in the minds of his

subjects. He can make them faithful and sincere only when he is kind and considerate, when he reduces their troubles and difficulties, when he does not oppress or tyrannize them, and when he never asks for things beyond their capacities.[156]

As one of our mentors once said, negative feedback should be treasured because it indicates where one can improve. Positive feedback, on the other hand, only reinforces the status quo. The above quotation from Ali (ra) also discusses how a leader can ensure that his followers are not self-serving.

Step 3. Enabling Others to Act

As mentioned earlier, leadership implies a social exchange process between leader and followers. Consequently, a leader must actively foster collaboration. It is the joint effort of leader and followers that make things happen, insha' Allah. To build collaboration among members, the leader needs to promote interaction among them as frequently as possible. Hold a membership meeting every two weeks. If you cannot hold such a meeting, still try to arrange for some form of regular group activity such as a Friday get-together to promote group bonding and cohesiveness. Kouzes and Posner point out that some organizations with superior leaders even hold a staff meeting every morning. Do not put a "prestige curtain" between you and your members.[157] Emphasize the long-term goals and benefits over short-run objectives and gains. Ensure that the goals of your organization require teamwork over individualistic efforts. Finally, collaboration can also be fostered by nurturing trusting relationships between yourself and your members.

When a leader trusts his members to take charge of a problem, this fact will energize them, and will lead them to come up with solutions that the leader may never have imagined. Members must be able to see their work as meaningful and significant, and must be encouraged to take ownership of a task or responsibility. An excellent example of what members can do when entrusted with responsibility comes from Motorola.[158] From 1987 through 1992, this global company was involved in training its workers to focus on quality. Hosain Rasoli was a technician involved with power transformers. Before the training program, he often asked himself how the transformers performed in the

---

[156] Loc. cit.

[157] Behzadnia and Denny, p. 21.

[158] Bolman and Deal, p. 345.

field. As part of the program, he was entrusted with improving the quality of the transformers. After gathering information about the weakest components of the transformer, he then convinced the development engineers to redesign the parts, resulting in a 400 percent improvement in the product's reliability. Rasoli is now "Mr. Power Amplifier" at Motorola.

Besides fostering collaboration, the leader must strengthen others. The key to strengthening others is through empowerment and delegation. Both concepts share the same idea: power is an expandable resource. The more power the leader gives to his members, the more influence he has, and the more he has strengthened his members. Consequently, any demand he makes of them is a demand that he makes of the whole group or organization. Thus, the example of Muhammad (saw) is of a leader who did what he had told others to do. The following hadith narrated by Abu Talhah demonstrates how the Prophet strengthened others when the Quraish imposed a ban on the Muslims:

> When we complained to Allah's Messenger (saw) of hunger and raised our clothes to show we were each carrying a stone over our bellies, Allah's Messenger (peace be upon him) raised his clothes and showed that he had two stones on his belly.[159]

While strengthening his members, the leader will also need to raise their level of commitment to the cause. As discussed in Chapter Six, delegation is critical here. The more members feel that they are personally responsible for a course of action, the more committed they feel. Some leaders use a "signing up" ritual whereby a person agrees to do his best for the project to succeed.[160] In the sīrah of the Prophet (saw), the first pledge of Aqaba can be viewed as an example of this commitment process.[161]

Another way of building up the commitment level of your members is by making choices visible to others. Have the member commit to performing a task in front of the group or committee. The more visible the choice, the more committed people are to that course of action. Simultaneously, guard against escalation to a previous course of action. Members who have committed themselves to a previous task may continue in that task even if the project is not working out and they keep

---

[159] Reported by Tirmidhi in *Mishkat*, copied from *The Islamic Scholar*.
[160] Kouzes and Posner, p. 226.
[161] Lings, p. 109.

receiving negative feedback.[162] If a member becomes too attached to a project that is continuously underperforming, rotate him out of the project, and assign somebody else to it. Simultaneously, the leader may assign the brother who was experiencing escalation to a project that fits him better.

Step 4. Modeling the Way

Amirs must not remain static after developing a shared vision and empowering others. They must model the way. First, they must be clear about their beliefs. By practicing what they preach, they make clear to their followers what core values and behavior should be emulated. The following hadith from *Sahih Bukhari* makes this clear:

> [Usama] heard Allah's Messenger saying, "A man will be brought and put in Hell (Fire) and he will circumambulate (go around and round) in Hell (Fire) like the donkey of a (flour) grinding mill. All the people of Hell (Fire) will gather around him and will say to him, 'O so-and-so! Didn't you use to order others for good and forbid them from evil?' That man will say, 'I used to order others to do good but I myself never used to do it, and I used to forbid others from evil while I myself used to do evil."[163]

Most importantly, the Prophet Muhammad (*saw*) modeled the way for his companions and is still the example all current Muslim leaders and followers should follow. Allah says the following about Muhammad (*saw*) in the Qur'an:

$$ وَ إِنَّكَ لَعَلَىٰ خُلُقٍ عَظِيمٍ $$

And lo! you are of an exalted character. (Qalam, 68:4)

While modeling the way, the leader must remember that the level of maturity of his followers will affect the degree and speed at which they follow his example. Because of differing levels of member maturity and the nature of the task, a leader must break down the goal into small, manageable chunks. As a result, he will be aiming for small wins. Small wins are important because they provide the members a sense of

---

[162] Bazerman, M., Beekun, R. and Schoorman, D. (1982). "Performance Evaluation in a Dynamic Context: A Laboratory Study of the Impact of a Prior Commitment to the Ratee." *Journal of Applied Psychology*, 67, 873–76.

[163] Reported by Abu Wail, *Sahih Bukhari*, 9:218.

accomplishment, give them self-confidence and thereby have a multiplier effect.[164]

Step 5. Encouraging the Heart

Succeeding in the path of Allah is difficult and Muslims will be continuously tested.   Sometimes, brothers and sisters may become discouraged. An appropriate *ayat* or hadith at a tough time will help refocus them and strengthen their resolve. The example of the Prophet Ya'qub (*as*) is an excellent reminder during trying times:

يَبَنِيَّ اذْهَبُواْ فَتَحَسَّسُواْ مِن يُوسُفَ وَ أَخِيهِ وَ لاَ تَايْـَسُواْ مِن رَّوْحِ اللَّهِ إِنَّهُ لاَ يَايْـَسُ مِن رَّوْحِ اللَّهِ إِلاَّ الْقَوْمُ الْكَـٰفِرُونَ

> O my sons! go and enquire about Joseph and his brother and never give up hope of Allah's soothing mercy: truly no one despairs of Allah's soothing mercy except those who have no faith. (Yusuf, 12:87)

Another *ayat* that is equally inspiring is:

وَلاَ تَهِنُواْ وَلاَ تَحْزَنُواْ وَأَنتُمُ ٱلأَعْلَوْنَ إِن كُنتُم مُّؤْمِنِينَ

> So lose not heart, nor fall into despair: For you must gain mastery if you are true in faith. (Al 'Imran, 3:139)

A dinner or some other form of recognition to thank everybody is also a very good way to thank the organizational members (and others) who have helped. People do not work for Allah's cause with a desire to gain recognition or earn material rewards, but a pat on the back can energize them for the road ahead. It is the leader's job to demonstrate to them that they can win with the help of Allah, *subhanahu wa ta'ala.*

The leaders should not wait until their projects are completely finished before encouraging their members. One of the most important tenets of

---

[164] Weick, K (1979). *The Social Psychology of Organizing.* Reading, MA: Addison-Wesley.

motivation is the Law of Effect: behavior that is rewarded will be repeated while behavior that is not rewarded will not be. Accordingly, leaders should establish targets along the path to long-term objectives. Whenever their members reach a target, they should celebrate their accomplishment so that they are encouraged to continue making progress.

In Focus 2: Khurram Murad —
A Visionary Leader among *Da'is*

Khurram Murad (1932–1996) was the former vice-president of Jamaat-e-Islami, Pakistan, the former director of the Islamic Foundation, UK, and a Qur'an scholar. A professional civil engineer, he was actively involved in the Islamic movement since 1948. Later he served as the President of Islami Jamiat Talaba, Pakistan, and became a member of the Central Executive of Jama'at Islami, Pakistan. A prolific writer, his works include: *Way to the Qur'an, Sacrifice: The making of a Muslim, Da'wah among Non-Muslims in the West, Muslim Youth in the West,* and translations of Maududi's works such as *Let Us Be Muslims* and *Witnesses unto Mankind: The Purpose and Duty of the Muslim Ummah.*

During his stay in the West, Murad expressed great concern about the assimilation of new converts into the Islamic society. In fact, it was at his prodding that Yusuf Islam (the recording artist formerly known as Cat Stevens) started making cassettes and CD's on *sīrah* of the Holy Prophet (*saw*). Another leading Muslim in the West, Ahmad Von Denffer worked with him at the Islamic Foundation, Leicester, from 1978 to 1984. In working with new converts, Murad was a great reservoir of patience, and always returned and referred to the Holy Qur'an for guidance. Simultaneously, he strove to bring cordiality among Muslim organizations. He worked very hard at mobilizing the Muslim youth, and urged them to break out of the cocoon of the self, and to become engaged as *da'is*.

Murad's thinking on what Muslims and Muslim leaders must do in the West crystallized around one visionary theme: the contextualization of the Islamic movement, and is summarized below:[165]

---

[165] Much of the material that follows is based on Murad's (1996) cassette series published posthumously, his introduction to Sayyid Abul A'la Maududi's *The Islamic Movement: Dynamics of Values, Power and Change* published by the Islamic Foundation in 1991, and Larry Poston's *Islamic Da'wah in the West* published by Oxford University Press in 1992.

- *Ultimate mission of the Islamic movement*: The Islamic Movement is "an organized struggle to change the existing society into an Islamic society based on the Qur'an and the Sunnah and to make Islam, which is a code for entire life, supreme and dominant, especially in the sociopolitical spheres."[166]

- *Leaders of the Islamic movement must not be constrained by "historical" Islam.* There is a difference between the Islam of the Qur'an and the Sunnah and the Islam of historical development. Historical Islam carries with it "[burdens] of misgiving and misunderstanding, of misperception and misrepresentation, of mistrust and hostility, of images, both false and true, which seem to have become permanently lodged in hearts and minds."[167] Murad suggests that Muslims should not allow themselves to be shackled by these aspects of their history. Indeed, Muslim leaders need not apologize for activities undertaken under the name of Islam since the time of the Prophet Muhammad (*saw*) and the four Rightly Guided Caliphs. If need be, they should repudiate whatever in their past that is against the Qur'an and Sunnah. This would be in the spirit of true *istighfar*.

يَـٰٓأَيُّـهَا ٱلَّذِينَ ءَامَنُواْ كُونُواْ قَوَّٰمِينَ بِٱلْقِسْطِ

شُهَدَآءَ لِلَّهِ وَلَوْ عَلَىٰٓ أَنفُسِكُمْ أَوِ ٱلْوَٰلِدَيْنِ وَٱلْأَقْرَبِينَ

إِن يَكُنْ غَنِيًّا أَوْ فَقِيرًا فَٱللَّهُ أَوْلَىٰ بِهِمَا فَلَا تَتَّبِعُواْ

ٱلْهَوَىٰٓ أَن تَعْدِلُواْ وَإِن تَلْوُۥٓاْ أَوْ تُعْرِضُواْ فَإِنَّ ٱللَّهَ

كَانَ بِمَا تَعْمَلُونَ خَبِيرًا

> O you who believe! stand out firmly for justice as witnesses to Allah even as against yourselves or your parents or your kin and whether it be (against) rich or poor: for Allah can best protect both. Follow not the lusts (of your hearts) lest you swerve and if you distort (justice) or decline to do justice verily

---

[166] Murad, K. (1981). *Islamic Movement in the West.* London: The Islamic Foundation, 1981, p. 3.
[167] Murad, K. *Da'wah among Non-Muslims in the West.* Leicester, UK: The Islamic Foundation, p. 18.

Allah is well-acquainted with all that you do.
(Nisaa, 4:135)

- *Local Muslims must be involved.* "[The] ultimate objective of the Islamic Movement shall not be realized until the struggle is made by the locals. For it is only they that have the power to change the society into an Islamic society."[168]

- *Communicate using the same frame of reference as the target audience.* Emulating the example of previous prophets, leaders must communicate in the same language as their followers or those whom they are doing *da'wah* to. Invite non-Muslims to something that they accept or something which follows from what they accept: worshipping the One God only:

قُلْ يَـٰٓأَهْلَ ٱلْكِتَـٰبِ تَعَالَوْاْ إِلَىٰ كَلِمَةٍ سَوَآءِ بَيْنَنَا وَ
بَيْنَكُمْ أَلَّا نَعْبُدَ إِلَّا ٱللَّهَ وَلَا نُشْرِكَ بِهِ شَيْئًا وَلَا يَتَّخِذَ
بَعْضُنَا بَعْضًا أَرْبَابًا مِّن دُونِ ٱللَّهِ فَإِن تَوَلَّوْاْ فَقُولُواْ
ٱشْهَدُواْ بِأَنَّا مُسْلِمُونَ

> Say: "O people of the Book! come to common terms as between us and you: that we worship none but Allah; that we associate no partners with Him; that we erect not from among ourselves lords and patrons other than Allah." If then they turn back say: "Bear witness that we (at least) are Muslims (bowing to Allah's will)." (Al 'Imran, 3:64)

Besides using a common frame of reference, Murad suggests that we use terminology that is more likely to strike a sympathetic cord in non-Muslims. Instead of calling for a ban on alcohol, Muslims may first seek to have harmful drugs such as heroin, cocaine, etc. banned. Later on, Muslims may work toward circumscribing alcohol.

- *Focus on contemporary issues.* The teachings of the Qur'an and the Prophet (*saw*) must be related to contemporary issues in a language that the addressee can understand. Murad's rationale is that "we can only make contemporary man hear and understand the Message of Allah through the words that he knows, in a language that he is

---

[168] Ibid., p. 36

familiar with."[169] Thus, the Prophet Nuh's[170] (*as*) message focused on the issue of caste and class differences; the Prophet Hud (*as*) took on imperialism; the Prophet Lut[171] (*as*) confronted permissiveness, and the Prophet Musa (*as*) challenged tyranny. Murad insists, therefore, that the message of Islam should be made relevant to the concerns of the day: abortion, drugs, the environment, nuclear proliferation, etc.

---

[169] Murad, K. Introduction to Maududi's *The Islamic Movement: Dyanmics of Values, Power and Change*, p. 15.

[170] Nuh (*as*) is the Arabic name of the Prophet Noah (*as*).

[171] Lut (*as*) is the Arabic name of the Prophet Lot (*as*).

Case Exercise: The Rose-Hill Islamic Association[172]

It is May 24, and the executive committee of the Rose-Hill Islamic Association is about to have a meeting. Rose-Hill is a multicultural city (see map on the next page), with a large Muslim community, an expansive depressed inner city area where Islam has been spreading rapidly, a small but wealthy group of "foreign" Muslims composed primarily of physicians and engineers, and a conservative non-Muslim community.

You are attempting to choose a site for the location of the Islamic Center of Rose-Hill. A map of the city of Rose-Hill is included on the next page. Three potential sites have been selected. One site is in the middle of the inner city where the greatest concentration of Muslims is located. The second site is located closer to the suburbs where the foreign Muslims live. So far these Muslims represent the major group of financial contributors to the new mosque project. The third site is closer to Rose-Hill State University, where many Muslim students reside. They have been praying in a rented apartment for the past few years. This rented apartment, which currently serves as the mosque for the city, will no longer be available in six months. The landlord has grown tired of complaints about noisy prayer sessions and Friday parking problems from his tenants. He has decided not to renew the lease on the apartment. Most of the people attending regular and *jumu'ah* prayers at this temporary mosque tend to be students too.

It is rumored that several large pledges of financial support may be withdrawn if the mosque committee does not make its decision today. Several meetings have taken place in the past, but have ended inconclusively. You have half an hour to make a decision and to place a phone call reporting your decision. You all agree when you set the meeting time that you can make your decision in half an hour.

Here are some of the people on the executive committee:

> Brother Zia, a graduate student in engineering, also acts as the imam of the temporary mosque.
>
> Sister Jihada, an American Muslim, is an activist in the community, and has done a lot of *da'wah*.

---

[172] The names of the Islamic association and all persons mentioned in the above case are fictitious. Any resemblance to any actual organization or living person is purely coincidental.

Brother 'Isa, a retired professor of English, is the secretary for public relations of the mosque.

Brother Muhammad is a licensed contractor who wants to be the builder chosen for the mosque construction project.

Brother 'Umar is from the inner city group, and is lobbying for the mosque to be built in his area with him as the imam.

Brother Yusuf is a wealthy consultant who has donated substantial amounts of money to community projects, but not to the mosque.

Step 1:

Participants should meet in groups of six in different parts of the room. You have 30 minutes to make a decision about the site of the new mosque. Each group participant should choose what role he or she wants to play, and then start the meeting.

Step 2:

Report your group's decision to the moderator.

Step 3:

Discussion with your workshop moderator.

Map of the City of Rose-Hill

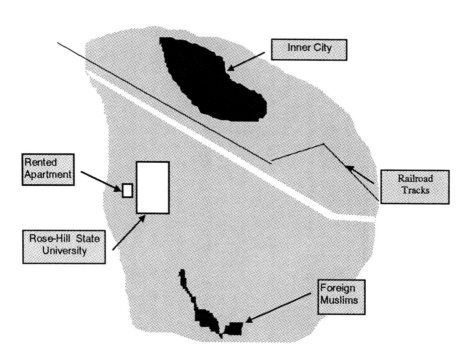

Conclusion

The task ahead is difficult, but essential to the survival of the Ummah. All great Islamic leaders have faced enormous struggles from within as well as from the outside: Muhammad (*saw*), Abu Bakr (*ra*), 'Umar (*ra*), 'Ali (*ra*), 'Uthman (*ra*), Fateh Sultan, Ismail Farooqi, Hassan Al-Banna, Syed Maudoodi, Malcolm X and so on. Often the solution has not been obvious, but all of them had one thing in common: the Islamic belief and its associated values.

None of these leaders, however, was intimidated by the task at hand. Just as every rainstorm starts with only one single drop of water, so too the renaissance of Islam has started with individual Muslims taking very simple, initial steps. The Ummah now needs unification and clear guidance. To reach the heights to which Islamic communities aspire, Islamic leaders — wherever they may be — must take simple, small steps at first. No road exists to take them there. With the help of Allah and a committed band of believers, each leader will have to step into the unknown first before anybody else to create and light up the path.

وَكَذَٰلِكَ جَعَلْنَٰكُمْ أُمَّةً وَسَطًا لِّتَكُونُوا شُهَدَآءَ عَلَى ٱلنَّاسِ وَيَكُونَ ٱلرَّسُولُ عَلَيْكُمْ شَهِيدًا وَمَا جَعَلْنَا ٱلْقِبْلَةَ ٱلَّتِى كُنتَ عَلَيْهَآ إِلَّا لِنَعْلَمَ مَن يَتَّبِعُ ٱلرَّسُولَ مِمَّن يَنقَلِبُ عَلَىٰ عَقِبَيْهِ وَإِن كَانَتْ لَكَبِيرَةً إِلَّا عَلَى ٱلَّذِينَ هَدَى ٱللَّهُ وَمَا كَانَ ٱللَّهُ لِيُضِيعَ إِيمَٰنَكُمْ إِنَّ ٱللَّهَ بِٱلنَّاسِ لَرَءُوفٌ رَّحِيمٌ

Thus have We made of you an Ummah justly balanced that you might be witnesses over the

nations and the Messenger a witness over
yourselves; and We appointed the *qiblah* to which
you were used only to test those who followed the
Messenger from those who would turn on their
heels (from the faith). Indeed it was (a change)
momentous except to those guided by Allah. And
never would Allah make your faith of no effect. For
Allah is to all people most surely full of kindness
Most Merciful. (Al Baqarah, 2:143)

Summary

1. Define leadership.

Leadership is the process of directing and influencing organizational
members so that they will take ownership of organizational activities
and programs.

2. What are the three sets of factors that underlie the leadership process?

The leadership process consists of transactions between leaders and
followers within a specific situational context. Hence, the three sets
of factors underlying this process are leader characteristics, follower
characteristics, and situational characteristics. A leader is effective to
the extent that there is a fit between his or her characteristics, the
characteristics of his or her followers, and the characteristics of the
situation.

3. List some Islamic characteristics that leaders should develop.

Building upon the bases of Islamic leadership, some of the attributes
that leaders should develop both in themselves and in their members
are: honesty, competence, being forward-looking, providing
inspiration, strength of character, humility, kindness and
magnanimity, being willing to seek consultation, equity and
impartiality, modesty and simplicity, and taking responsibility for
their members.

4. What follower characteristics affect a leader's effectiveness?

Two key characteristics have been emphasized in the Qur'an and the
sīrah of the Prophet Muhammad (*saw*): obedience and the willingness

to work in unity. The notion of *dynamic followership* is also important here.

5. Identify the different types of followers that a leader has to work with.

Followers can be classified by their level of critical thinking and dynamism. There are five types of followers in any Islamic organization: alienated followers, effective followers, indifferent followers, "yes" people, and "survivors." Although followers are not homogeneous, a leader cannot turn anybody away; rather, he needs to take everybody at their word, and work with them according to their aptitudes. *Gradualism* describes the process whereby a follower is gradually nurtured to attain his or her full potential.

6. Identify the situational characteristics that may affect a leader's effectiveness.

These are leader-member relationships, task structure, work-group characteristics, the organization's climate, its policies, and the maturity level of its members. A leader may be very effective in one situation, but rather ineffective in another.

7. Describe the leadership styles that a leader would rely upon when dealing with a variety of members across differing situations.

Assuming a leader can vary his style of leadership, there are four such leadership styles: supporting, coaching, delegating, and directive. An effective leader is one who can adjust his style of leadership to fit the characteristics of his members and the situation.

8. Describe how a leader can become an effective coach or mentor.

When acting as a coach, a leader is involved in a day-to-day, hands on set of activities geared toward helping members identify opportunities that can improve their capabilities and performance. The role of coaching involves three distinct roles: manager, evaluator, and coach. In acting as coach, the leader must create a nonthreatening and growth climate. He must also develop five critical skills: observation, analysis, delegation, interviewing, and feedback.

9. According to Kouzes and Posner's model of leadership effectiveness, what are the five steps a leader should follow in order to enhance the performance of members?

While trusting in Allah, these five steps are:

1. Challenging the process,
2. Inspiring a shared vision,
3. Enabling others to act,
4. Modeling the way, and
5. Encouraging the heart.

Glossary of Terms[173]

'Adl:	Justice, equilibrium, and equity. A fundamental value governing all social behavior and forming the basis of all social dealings and legal frameworks. Its antonym is *ẓulm* (injustice or inequity).
Akhirah:	Hereafter.
Alaihi Salām (*as*):	May Allah's peace be upon him.
Al Amīn:	The *Amīn* or the Trustworthy — a name given to Muhammad (*saw*) before he received *wahy*.
Al hamdu lillah:	Praise be to Allah.
Allah:	Creator and Sustainer of all. Supreme Being. The Arabic name "Allah" is not derived from any source.
'Amal Ṣalih:	Good deeds.
Amānah :	Something given to someone for safekeeping. Trust.
Amir:	Leader
Ansār:	Helpers – collective title of the people of Madinah who helped the Prophet and his Companions when they migrated from Makkah to Madinah.
'Asabiyyah:	A concept where people put the needs of their group or clan ahead of the needs of the whole community.
Awqāf:	A trusteeship.
Ayat:	A section of the text of the Qur'an referred to as a "verse." It literally means a sign, indication or message.
'Azm:	Resolve.

---

[173] Based on an integration of definitions from glossaries in *Islamic Scholar* software, *Taqwa: The provision of believers* (London: Al Firdous, 1996), and Dr. Taha Jabir al Awani's *Ethics of Disagreement in Islam* (Herndon, VA: International Institute of Islamic Thought, 1994).

Bay'ah:	A pledge of allegiance.
Bayt al Māl:	The Muslim public treasury.
Bid'ah:	Literally an innovation. In Islam, it means an innovative act that is carried out on the assumption that it has Islamic validity when it doesn't in fact. Refers to any act that has no precedent from, or no continuity with, the Sunnah.
Caliph:	The leader of the Muslim Ummah.
Da'wah:	Invitation; call. Refers to the duty of Muslims to invite or call others (both Muslims and non-Muslims) to the straight and natural path of Islam or submission to Allah.
Dīn:	Religion, but more, a way of life. Used to refer to Islam and the way of life it ordains.
Dinars:	Money/coins.
Du'a:	Supplication to Allah. Invocation.
Dunya:	World/Earth.
Fi Sabil lillah:	In the way of Allah. For Allah's Cause.
Hadith:	Lit., an account. Narrations and reports of the deeds and sayings of the Holy Prophet (*saw*).
Hajj:	Pilgrimage during the month of Dhu al Hijjah to Makkah where the Ka'bah, the House of Allah, is located.
Halāl:	Anything permitted by the Shari'ah (Islamic Law). Lawful.
Haqq:	Right.
Hijrah:	Migration of the Holy Prophet from Makkah to Madinah. To leave one's place of residence either for the sake of Allah or some other reason. The Muslim calendar begins from the year of the Hijrah of the Prophet (A.D. 622). Also the act of leaving a bad practice in order to adopt a righteous way of life.
Hikmah:	One's ability to put knowledge (*ilm*) into practice.
Hudūd:	The limits set by Allah that should not be trespassed; the mandatory punishments assigned by the Qur'an and the Sunnah for particular crimes.

Ihsān:	Lit., doing good or excelling. One of the highest degrees of *imān* (faith), where one serves Allah as if one is seeing Him, and though one cannot see Him, still one knows that Allah sees him.
'Ilm:	Knowledge.
Imām:	A person who is leading any of the five prayers that Muslims observe daily. It also means a leader in general, a reputable scholar, or the leader of a Muslim country.
Imān:	Belief in the articles of faith enunciated in the Qur'an and the Sunnah.
Insha' Allah:	God willing.
Islam:	Lit., to submit and offer peace. The religion of submission to the will of Allah. The religion of Muslims.
Jahiliyyah:	The age of ignorance. The name given to the later period between the Prophet 'Isa (*as*) and the Prophet Muhammad (*saw*) when people forgot the teachings of the prophets, and violated the religious sanctities.
Jam'ah:	Congregation, community or group of Muslims.
Jihad:	Lit., to struggle. "Any earnest striving in the way of Allah, involving either personal effort, material resources, or arms for righteousness and against evil, wrongdoing, and oppression. Where it involves armed struggle, it must be for the defense of the Muslim community or to protect non-Muslims from evil, oppression, and tyranny."[174]
Ka'bah:	A cube-shaped building built by the Prophets Ibrahim and Ismail (*as*), the first house built for the worship of Allah. Situated in Makkah, the direction all Muslims face when praying .
Khalifah:	Steward, vicegerent, succesor. Man is referred to in the Qur'an (Baqarah, surah 2, verse 30) as the *khalifah* or steward of Allah on earth. "The word *khalifah* was used after the death of the Prophet Muhammad (*saw*) to refer to his successor , Abu Bakr (*ra*), as head of the Muslim community. Later,

---

[174] Ibid., p. 141.

	it came to be accepted as the designation for the head of the Muslim state. Anglicized as Caliph."[175]
Khutbah:	Sermon, especially during the Friday prayer. During key Islamic festivals, congregrational prayers take place when a *khutbah* is given.
Kufr:	Lit., covering, hiding or being ungrateful. In Islam, it means rejecting any or all articles of faith.
Madinah:	The city in Arabia where the Prophet Muhammed (*saw*) is buried. The city of the Holy Prophet (*saw*) in Arabia.
Makkah:	The city in Arabia where the Holy Ka'bah is situated.
Masjid:	Place of worship.
Mount al Ṣafa:	A hilltop in Makkah, by the sacred mosque.
Muhājirīn:	Migrators, emigrants. Title given to the Muslims who, along with the Prophet, migrated from Makkah to Madinah. Singular is *muhājir*.
Muhsinīn:	Used to describe those who bear the qualities of *ihsān*, i.e., those who do good or excel.
Mu'min:	One who has *imān* (plural *mu'minīn*).
Munāfiqīn:	Hypocrites.
Muslim:	Believers in one God and the Prophet Muhammad (*saw*). One who submits to the Will of God.
Muttaqīn:	Those who have *taqwa* or fear of Allah.
Qiblah:	The direction (toward the Ka'bah in Makkah) all Muslims must face when performing *ṣalāh* from any given point on earth.
Qur'an:	The final book or revelation from Allah to mankind, revealed to the Prophet Muhammad (*saw*) over a span of 23 years.
Raḍi Allahu 'anhu (m.) **Raḍi Allahu 'anha** (f.)	(*ra*): May Allah be pleased with him or her.
Ramaḍan:	Ninth month of the Islamic Calendar during which Muslims fast dawn to dusk.
Rasūl Allah:	Messenger of Allah (Prophet Muhammad) (*saw*).

---

[175] Al 'Awani, p. 141.

Ṣadiq:	The truthful — a name given to Muhammad (*saw*) before he received *wahy*.
Ṣabr:	Observing patience.
Ṣahaba:	Companions of the Prophet Muhammad (*saw*) during his life.
Ṣahīh:	Lit., sound. Technically, a hadith whose chain of narrators is authentic in belief, character, and memory.
saw:	Abbreviated words of honor and salutations attached to the name of the Holy Prophet Muhammad (*saw*). Meaning: May Allah send blessings and salutations on him.
Sīrah:	Lit., conduct. The study of the life of the Prophet (*saw*).
Shari'ah:	Lit., a path. It is used to mean Islam's legal system that Muslims abide by.
Shūra:	Consultative process of decision making
Sunnah:	Lit., a tradition or practice. The body of traditions and practices of the Prophet (*saw*); also includes his words, actions, or what has been approved by him.
Tafsīr:	Commentary or exegesis. The science of explaining and commenting on the verses of the Qur'an.
Taif:	A city in Saudi Arabia.
Taqwa:	Piety — fear or consciousness of Allah.
Tarbiyyah:	Training toward self-development.
Tawhid:	Belief in or affirmation of the absolute Oneness of Allah.
Tazkiyyah:	Growth.
Ummah:	Refers to the community of believers worldwide, irrespective of color, race, language, nationality, or boundaries. The universal body of Muslims as a single community.
Wahy:	Revelation from Allah.
Wudhu:	Obligatory ablution or washing before *salāh* (prayer) and other acts.

Yaqīn: Conviction in Allah's signs.

Yathrib: The name of Madinah before the Prophet Muhammad
                               (*saw*) migrated to it.

Zakah: The amount payable by a Muslim on his net worth as
                               a part of his religious obligation, mainly for the
                               benefit of the poor and the needy.

Ẓulm: A comprehensive term used to refer to all forms of
                               inequity, injustice, exploitation, oppression, and
                               wrongdoing, whereby a person either deprives others
                               of their rights or does not fulfil his obligations toward
                               them.

Bibliography

1. Abu Dawud (1996). *Sunan* in *Winalim*. Silver Springs, MD: ISL Software Corporation, Release 4.

2. Al 'Awani, Tahir Jabir (1993). *The Ethics of Disagreement in Islam*. Herndon, VA: International Institute of Islamic Thought.

3. Al Buraey, Muhammad (1985). *Administrative Development: An Islamic Perspective*. London, UK: KPI.

4. Al Habshi, Syed Othman (1987) "Development of Islamic Managerial and Administrative Practices: A Historical Perspective." In *Seminar on Islamic Management*. Edited by the Training Division of the Islamic Research and Training Institute. Malaysia, Kuala Lumpur.

5. Al Hilali, Muhammad Taqi-ud and Khan, Muhammad Muhsin (1989). *The Interpretation of the Meanings of the Noble Qur'an: A Summarized Version of Al Tabari, Al Qurtubi, and Ibn Kathir with Comments from Sahih Al Bukhari*. Translation. Lahore, Pakistan: Kazi Publications.

6. Ali, Abdullah Yusuf (1989). *The Holy Qur'an: Text, Translation and Commentary*. Beltville, MD: Amana Corporation.

7. Altalib, Hisham (1993). *Training Guide for Islamic Workers*. Herndon, VA: IIIT and IIFSO.

8. Asad, M. (1985). *The Principles of State and Government in Islam*. Gibraltrar: Dar Al Andalus.

9. Al Suyuti, Jalal al Din (1996). *The History of the Khalifahs Who Took the Right Way*. Translation of *Tarikh al Khulafa* by 'Abdassamad Clarke. London: Ta-Ha Publishers.

10. Barboza, S. (1994). *American Jihad: Islam after Malcolm X*. New York: Doubleday.

11. Bazerman, Max, Beekun, Rafik and Schoorman, David (1982). "Performance Evaluation in a Dynamic Context: A Laboratory Study of the Impact of a Prior Commitment to the Ratee." *Journal of Applied Psychology*, 67: 873–76.

12. Beekun, Rafik (1997). *Islamic Business Ethics*. Herndon, VA: IIIT.

13. Behzadnia, A. A. and Denny, S. *To the Commander in Chief from Imam Ali to Malik-E-Ashter.*

14. Bennis, Warren (1988). *Fortune* January.

15. Bolman, Lee G. and Deal, Terrence E. (1997). *Reframing Organizations: Artistry, Choice and Leadership.* San Francisco, CA: Jossey Bass.

16. Conger, J. A. (1990). *The Dark Dide of Leadership, Organizational Dynamics.* New York, NY: American Management Association. Autumn.

17. Davis, K. (1967). *Human Relations at Work: The Dynamics of Organizational Behavior.* New York. NY: McGraw-Hill.

18. Engel, Herbert. M. (1990) *How to Delegate: A Guide to Getting Things Done.* Houston, TX.

19. Faqih, I. (1988). *Glimpses of Islamic History.* Delhi, India: Adam Publishers and Distributors.

20. Fiedler, F. E. (1967). *A Theory of Leadership Effectiveness.* New York, NY: McGraw-Hill.

21. Finch, Raymond C. (1997). "Emerging Threats a Face of Future Battle Chechen Fighter Shamil Basayev." U.S. Army, Foreign Military Studies Office, Fort Leavenworth, KS·

22. Fisher, J. and Cole, K. (1993) *Leadership and Management of Volunteer Programs.* San Francisco: Jossey-Bass.

23. French, J. R. P. and Raven, B. (1959). "The Bases of Social Power." In Dorwin Cartwright (ed.), *Studies in Social Power.* Ann Arbor, Mich.: University of Michigan, pp. 150–167.

24. Gersick, C. J. G. (1988). "Time and Transition in Work Teams: Toward a New Model of Group Development." *Academy of Management Review,* March: 9–41.

25. Gibson, J. L., Ivancevich, J. M. and Donnelly, J. H. (1994). *Organizations: Behavior, Structure and Processes.* Burr Ridge, Ill: Irwin.

26. Greene, C. N. (1975). "The Reciprocal Nature of Influence between Leader and Subordinate." *Journal of Applied Psychology,* 60: 187–193.

27. Greenleaf, Robert (1970). *The Servant as Leader.* Indianapolis, IN: Greenleaf Center for Servant-Leadership.

28. Hamid, AbulWahid (1995). *Companions of the Prophet.* Leicester, UK: MELS, Volumes 1 and 2.

29. Haykal, M. H. (1976). *The Life of Muhammad (saw).* Indianapolis: IN, American Trust Publications.

30. Hellriegel, Don and Slocum, John (1992). *Management.* Reading, Mass: Addison-Wesley.

31. Hersey, P. and Blanchard, K. H. (1988). *Management of Organizational Behavior,* 5th edition. Englewood Cliffs, NJ: Prentice-Hall.

32. Hinkin, Timothy R. and Schriescheim, Chester (1988). "Power and Influence: The View from Below." *Personnel*, May: 47–50.

33. Hollander, E. P. (1978). *Leadership Dynamics*. New York, NY: Free Press.

34. Jabnoun, Naceur (1994). *Islam and Management.* Kuala Lumpur, Malaysia: Institut Kajian Dasar (IKD).

35. Khan, Muhammad W. (1998). "Prophetic Principles of Success." *Minaret* September: 8–9.

36. Kouzes, J. and Posner, B. (1995). *The Leadership Challenge: How to Get Extraordinary Things Done in Organizations*. San Francisco, CA: Jossey-Bass.

37. Kram, K. E. (1983). "Phases of the Mentor Relationship." *Academy of Management Journal,* December.

38. Lings, Martin (1983). *Muhammad: His Life Based on the Earliest Sources.* Rochester, VT: Inner Traditions International.

39. Maudoodi, Sayyid, Abu A'la (1991). *The Islamic Movement: Dynamics of Values, Power and Change.* Edited by Khurram Murad. Leicester, UK: The Islamic Foundation.

40. McCall, Jr., M. (1978). Power, Influence, and Authority: The Hazards of Carrying a Sword. Technical Report. Greensboro, NC: Center for Creative Leadership.

41. McClelland, D. (1961). *The Achieving Society*. Princeton, NJ: Van Nostrand.

42. *Mishkat al Masabih*, Islamic Scholar Software. (1996) South Africa: Johannesburg.

43. Murad, Khurram (1996). "Islamic Movement Theory and Practice: A Course for Those Striving for Islamic Change in the West." Young Muslims, Leicester, United Kingdom, Talk 9.

44. Murad, Khurram. (1986) *Da'wah among Non-Muslims in the West.* Leicester, UK: The Islamic Foundation.

45. Murad, Khurram (1981). *Islamic Movement in the West*. Leicester, UK: The Islamic Foundation.

46. Nahavandi, A. (1997). *The Art and Science of Leadership*. Upper Saddle River, NJ: Prentice-Hall.

47. Par Excellence Computers. (1996). "Prominent Muslims," Islamic Scholar Software. South Africa: Johannesburg.

48. Pickthall, Muhammad Marmaduke. *The Meaning of the Glorious Qur'an: Text and Explanatory Translation.*

49. Poston, Larry (1992). *Islamic Da'wah in the West.* New York: Oxford University Press.

50. Rahman, Afzalur. (1990) *Muhammad as a Military Leader*. Lahore, Pakistan: Islamic Publications.

51. Safi, Louay (1995). "Leadership and Subordination: An Islamic Perspective." *American Journal of Islamic Social Sciences,* Summer, vol. 12, 2: 204–223.

52. *Sahih Bukhari.* Islamic Scholar Software (1996). Johannesburg, South Africa: Par Excellence Computers.

53. *Sahih Muslim.* Islamic Scholar Software (1996). Johannesburg, South Africa: Par Excellence Computers.

54. Schein, E. H. (1997). *Organizational Culture and Leadership.* 2nd edition. San Francisco, CA: Jossey-Bass.

55. Schriescheim, C. A., Tolliver, J. M. and Behling, O. C. (1978). "Leadership Theory: Some Implications for Managers." *MSU Topics,* Summer (26): 35.

56. Senge, Peter (1990). *The Fifth Discipline.* New York: Currency Doubleday.

57. Shibli-Nu'mani, Shamsul 'Ulama A. (1957). *Omar the Great: The Second Caliph of Islam.* Vols. 1 and 2, 2nd Revision. Translated by Maulana Zafar Ali Khan. Pakistan: Lahore, Sh. Muhammad Ashraf.

58. Specter, Michael (1996). How Chechens Surprised Russian Foes to Recapture Capital. *The New York Times,* August 18.

59. Steinmetz, Lawrence L. (1976). *The Art and Skill of Delegation.* Reading, Mass: Addison-Wesley

60. Stogdill, R. M. (1974). *Handbook of Leadership: A Survey of Theory and Research.* New York: Free Press.

61. Stoner, James (1978). *Management.* Englewood Cliffs, NJ: Prentice-Hall, p. 441.

62. Thompson, A. and Strickland, A. (1993). *Strategic Management: Concepts and Cases.* Ill: Burr Ridge.

63. Umar-ud-din, Muhammad (1991). *The Ethical Philosophy of al Ghazzali.* Lahore, Pakistan: Sh. Muhammad Ashraf.

64. Weick, K. (1979). *The Social Psychology Of Organizing.* Reading, Mass: Addison-Wesley.

65. Wilkinson, H. (1993). *Influencing People in Organizations.* Fort Worth: The Dryden Press.

66. *Winalim* (1996). Silver Springs, MD: ISL Software, Release 4.

Index

‘

'*Adl* or Justice, 26, 27
'*Ahd* or keeping promise, 33

A

Abu Bakr, 39, 42, 43, 45, 68, 81, 131, 137
Abu Dawud, Bassaam, 105, 106
Abuse, 12
Accountability, 20, 22, 90
Ahwad, Nihad, viii
Ahzab, Battle of, 20, 44
al Nakha'i, Malik al Ashtar, 44
Alcohol, 65, 126
Al-Ghazzali, 26, 144
Amana, vii, 28, 29, 39, 109, 110
Ansar, 12, 40, 135
Asabiyyah, 117, 135
Authority, 8, 9, 10, 12, 14, 22, 39, 45, 49, 56, 79, 80, 89, 90, 100, 106, 143. *See* power

B

Badr, Battle of, 40, 42, 61, 62, 96
Barriers, 93
Basayev, Shamil, 142
Bases, moral, 17
Bennis, Warren, 8, 142
Bint Utbah, Hind, 64
Birr
    Righteousness, 29
Birr or righteousness, 30

C

CAIR
    Council on American Islamic Relations, viii, 116
Case Exercise, 128
Character, strength of, 18, 19, 25, 38, 43, 48, 86, 101, 122, 132
Charismatic, 9, 13, 14
Climate, 54, 73, 75, 76, 133
Closed system, 119
Coach, 2, 7, 68, 69, 75, 76, 77, 78, 79, 80, 82, 83, 100, 133
Coaching, 2, 47, 67, 68, 75, 76, 77, 78, 82, 83, 84, 105, 112, 133

G

H

I

J

K

L

M

N

O